The College Dorm Survival Guide

"As soon as you... colle... ...ut to get a copy of **The College Dorm** ...Sur...al Gui... ...ne ...... answers all your questions, even some you haven't thought about yet. You'll find down-to-earth information and really helpful advice from college grads as well as residence hall staff about everything dorm-related—from decorating to dealing with conflict."

—Harriet S. Mosatche, Ph.D., author of *Where Should I Sit at Lunch? The Ultimate 24/7 Guide to Surviving the High School Years*

"This guide is a must-have for the college-bound senior. I enthusiastically recommend it as a graduation gift for students and parents!"

—Jeff Stahlman, college counselor, New Albany High School

"For most students, college is the first time you'll be away from your parents. While you'll probably love the independence, you'll also gain a rapid lesson in cohabiting, relating, and learning just how different a roommate can be from you. This book is everything that you need to cope in your new environment. From adjusting to sleeping patterns to your roommate's practically live-in boyfriend, it offers practical advice to help you through the rough patches. You'll love Julia's writing style—she talks to you, not down to you. You'll also appreciate the real-life examples she shares from students who have been there and done that. It is a must-have for every college student—and for every parent who wants to help prepare their child for dorm life. If you plan to live in the dorm or even just with a roommate, you need this book!"

—Kelly Tanabe, coauthor of *Sallie Mae How to Pay for College: A Practical Guide for Families*

ALSO BY JULIA DEVILLERS

Girlwise:
How to Be Confident, Capable,
Cool, and In Control

How My Private, Personal Journal
Became a Bestseller

The Limited Too Tuned In
Series

The College Dorm Survival Guide

How to Survive and Thrive in Your New Home Away from Home

Julia DeVillers

Three Rivers Press
NEW YORK

Library of Congress Cataloging-in-Publication Data
DeVillers, Julia.
The college dorm survival guide : how to survive
and thrive in your new home away from home /
Julia DeVillers.— 1st ed.
1. Dormitories.   2. Dormitories—Social aspects.
3. Interpersonal relations.   4. College students.   I. Title.
LB3607.D47 2006
378.1'987—dc22   2005025336

ISBN 13: 978-0-7615-2674-2
ISBN 10: 0-7615-2674-9

Printed in the United States of America

Design by Karen Minster

10   9   8   7   6   5   4   3

First Edition

TO
JULIE PHILLIPS,
RESIDENCE HALL PRO

CONTENTS

THE COLLEGE DORM SURVIVAL GUIDE

INTRODUCTION

Move to a dorm, and your life will never be the same again.

Sound dramatic?

Yeah.

Is it true?

Yeah.

Think about it.

BEFORE: You live with your mom, dad, or other parental units. Maybe some sisters, brothers, pets, etc.

DORM: You live with hundreds or thousands of complete strangers.

BEFORE: You share a bedroom with a brother or sister . . . or nobody.

DORM: You share a bedroom with a complete stranger. Maybe two of them. Maybe even more.

BEFORE: You share a bathroom with a couple of people.

DORM: You share a bathroom with a ton of complete strangers.

BEFORE: Parent does your laundry. Parent provides food. Parent tells you what time to be home. Parent gives you punishment when you mess up.

DORM: It's all up to . . . you.

Living in a dorm is a completely unique experience. It's often the first time you live away from home, and all of a sudden you're rooming with hundreds or even thousands of people your age with different personalities and from different backgrounds.

It can be fun. Or not.

It's not always easy to live in a dorm. Most students are thrown into dorm living with little information about how to succeed or even what to expect. Some people seem to catch on quickly, but behind most freshman faces is a person going, "Um, huh?"

Mom may tell you not to mix your red shirt with your white socks in the laundry, but who will tell you how to mix with your new floormates? Your older cousin may tell you about the Freshman 15, but who will tell you about the 15 things freshmen can do to avoid it?

What to bring for your room
   (and what *not* to bring!)

Dealing with annoying roommates!

Decorating your room!

Romance!

Homesickness!

Sharing bathrooms with strangers!

Who will tell you what you need to know about surviving—and thriving—in the dorms?

The College Dorm Survival Guide will.

Within these pages you'll learn all about dorm life from people who have been there and done that. Things have really changed, even just over the past few years, and you need to know all the new ins and outs of dorm life. For one thing, in the college world, DORMS AREN'T CALLED *DORMS* anymore. And all the knowledgeable Residence Life contributors in this book will be the first to tell you that. Dorm: The old stereotype of a tiny gray cubicle with a bed and a desk and not much else to offer. Residence hall: Soooo much more. (But okay, the term *dorm* is catchy, and it works in this title so we all know what the book is about.)

Read on to see why, and to see how to get the most out of . . .

. . . your new home.

1

WELCOME TO YOUR NEW HOME

The day you enter your college dorm, your life changes. This is no ordinary experience you're signing up for. It's bizarre. A whole lot of people, pretty much the same age, all living together. You'll meet strangers who will become your friends (or not). You'll share late-night talks and early morning classes. You'll have a space to share, decorate, and turn into home for nine months out of the year. And, most important of all, you'll learn something new every single day because of the people and experiences you can only find in the dorms.

Where else can you find hundreds, and sometimes thousands, of similar-aged people living in close quarters, sharing not only residential space, but also social areas, meal times, classes, and countless other growth opportunities?

—Joan Schmidt, associate director of Residence Life at Central Michigan University and past president of the Association of College and University Housing Officers-International (ACUHO-I)

Life doesn't get better than a bus at your front door, three meals a day, an endless array of friends, and no utility bills to pay.

—Tosha Jansen-Conkey, senior at University of Kansas

YOUR DORM-I-TUDE

There are tons of different dorms and tons of people with different attitudes and personalities about to move into each one. How do you feel about moving to the dorms?

a. Yeah! COLLEGE! Freedom! I don't care what my dorm is like—I'm freeeee!

b. I'm an introvert. Not used to having all these people around. But I'll give it a shot.

c. Study, study, books, books . . . where's the study carrel? Which way to the library?

d. Okay. I've lived at home all my life. Some sleepovers. One week at Scout sleepaway camp. WTF? I'm cool. I'm legally an adult. I can handle this. This is weird. That guy looks weird. That RA is a little too perky. That girl looks kinda cool. This is surreal. I'm here. Now what?

Basically, most students go in hoping and expecting the best of their dorm experience. And that's great. Go in expecting *perfection,* though, and you're going to be disappointed. Living in your house wasn't perfect, right? Dorm life won't be, either—and that's to be expected. In a way it's not natural to suddenly be sharing your home with total strangers. It can be really, really fun. Really, really exciting. Just go in realizing that it's also *hard* to adjust to living in a dorm—and that's okay.

When you first get to campus, you'll probably want to immediately leave the dorm and meet lots of people and make connections, right? Well, you might want to reconsider. Of course you should meet people, but having a roommate and sharing a bathroom can be a really valuable part of the college experience. It will teach you how to share your space with others, and it also leads to some serious bonding. Some lifelong friendships can be made over sharing a cramped room or common area.

WHAT'S A DORM?

Throughout this book, you'll notice that the terms *dorm* and *residence hall* are used pretty much interchangeably. *Dorm* comes from *dormitory,* which has traditionally been a place where students just eat and sleep. The word *dormitory* can make you think of a small, dingy, sterile room. *So* not pleasant.

However, people who live and work in the college environment use the term *residence halls* now. That's because today's "dorms" are so much more than they used to be. They're places where you can become part of a community, interact with faculty, hang with your neighbors, and learn new things. It sounds way more appealing—and it is.

THE RIGHT DORM FOR YOU

Dorms have different living arrangements, different personalities, different reputations. Dorms can have their own culture, history, traditions, and even their own values. During orientation or an Admissions tour, you may hear that one dorm is the party dorm, one's the geek dorm, one's the Greek dorm . . .

As a freshman, you usually go where they put you. Some colleges have lotteries and you take your chances.

Some colleges let you make requests. Sometimes you'll even get your request. More likely? You won't.

This was the scene at my precollege orientation when we got our dorm assignments:

CUTE GUY: @#$#, I'm in the loser dorm!
NON-PARTY-GIRL GIRL: @#$#, I'm in the party dorm!
STUCK-UP-LOOKING GIRL: @#$#%, I'm in the way-out-in-the-middle-of-nowhere dorm!
PUNK GIRL: @#$#, I'm in the preppy dorm!
NON-JOCK GUY: @$#%, I'm in the jock dorm!
ME: YEAH! I got the dorm I requested! YEAH!!!

Jump forward one year later: I moved to the way-out-in-the-middle-of-nowhere dorm that turned out to be really fun—rooming with the stuck-up-looking girl, who turnd out to be my new best friend. The dorm I requested, which I lived in as a freshman, didn't turn out to be the best fit for me.

The moral is: Don't freak when you get your dorm assignment, even if it's not your first choice. Keep an open mind.

Don't let the building's reputation become a self-fulfilling prophecy. Dorms can change every year with a new crop of freshmen, especially because many of them didn't choose the dorm but were placed there, just like you. The "study dorm" can change to the "Greek dorm" if a lot of the freshmen pledge. The "Greek dorm" can change to the "study dorm" if a lot of the fraternity brothers move to their fraternity houses. So, if you're more of a homebody and get placed in the "party dorm," don't think you have to rise to the challenge and live up to that reputation.

Chances are that you'll find other students living all around you who think the hard-partying life is overrated, too. Or if it's the reverse, you might find a lot of people you can study with and relax with, but there will definitely be other people you can bond with over the nightlife.

SO MANY CHOICES

These days, there are hundreds of choices when it comes to types of dorms. Schools are building like crazy and renovating existing spaces to meet students' needs.

If you want to know more about the different dorms, check them out beforehand. Walk through some when you're touring the campus. Or go online. Many schools have pictures, descriptions, even virtual tours of the rooms on their websites.

If you try to make a request for a specific dorm, consider other factors besides reputation, says Katie Boone, the director of Housing and Residential Services at the Catholic University of America in Washington, D.C. Consider:

- Do you want to be close to the library so you'll be more inclined to go there?
- Will things like pool tables in common lounges be an attraction or a distraction?
- Does a dorm with a particular theme appeal to you?
- Are you looking for a quieter environment?
- Do you want to be close to a gym or fitness facility?
- Do you want to be close to a certain building because of your major?

DORM OPTIONS

BIG HALLS

Some residence halls are like small cities. Huge. The largest, the Jester Center at the University of Texas at Austin, is a million-plus square feet and has beds for three thousand students.

PROS: When hundreds of students live together, your chances of finding people you click with rise exponentially. There's always something to do: Large buildings typically have a lot going on, from activities to hall government to a party at any given time. Tall buildings have great views. And climbing stairs can be good exercise.

CONS: It can sometimes be easy to get lost in the shuffle of so many students. It can feel overwhelming and impersonal. There might be long waits for elevators, gym equipment, etc. You'll have long walks upstairs if the elevators break. Some high-rises are very high—if you're afraid of heights, request to be placed elsewhere.

SMALL HALLS

Small halls usually house under a hundred people. They might look like houses or apartment buildings. They might even *be* houses or small apartment buildings.

PROS: Small dorms often have a cozy, homelike feel to them, and sometimes the amenities are nicer. You may feel closer to your fellow dormmates. You'll probably know your hall director on a first-name basis, too.

CONS: There may not be as much variety of people to meet. Fewer activities. And, like living in a small town, more people will know your business.

FIRST-YEAR-EXPERIENCE HALLS

These halls are for freshmen or new students only. They often have special programs and services to help ease you into college life.

PROS: Living completely among first-year students who are all going through what you are can be reassuring. Everyone is new, so everyone hasn't cliqued off yet. And the programs the dorm offers specifically for you can be really beneficial.

CONS: Everyone's about your age, so you'll have little or no guidance from experienced upperclassmen. Living in these dorms may result in "freshmen gone wild" syndrome.

MIXED-YEAR HALLS

These dorms have a mix of lower- and upper-grade students. Freshmen may live next door to seniors or even in the same room.

PROS: Here you'll find more variety of ages. New students can benefit from the wisdom and experience of others.

CONS: New freshmen can feel overwhelmed living with seasoned pros. Cliques already in place can leave freshmen out. Older students can prey on freshman inexperience.

COEDUCATIONAL HOUSING

Most dorms mix up guys and girls. They might live right next door to each other or on separate areas of the same floor, or floors might alternate all-girl and all-guy.

PROS: In coed dorms, you'll have the opportunity to get to know students of both sexes, making it more like the "real world." It's a good way to learn to be comfortable with the opposite sex, especially for people who don't have siblings of the other gender.

CONS: Some people may feel the need to impress the opposite sex, which can result in fashion traumas or hall dramas. And there's always the possibility of hookups gone wrong.

· ·

REALLLLY COED

It's extremely rare and incredibly controversial, but a handful of the most liberal schools around the country have extended coeducational housing beyond buildings and floors to include actual sharing of rooms, making for some of the most liberal dormitory policies. Haverford College (PA), Swarthmore (PA), Wesleyan University (CT), and Hampshire College (MA) allow men and women to live together.

· ·

ALL-MALE OR ALL-FEMALE HOUSING

Some halls only house people of one gender. Some think it's old-fashioned; others enjoy the benefits.

PROS: Many people feel more comfortable in a single-gender dorm, especially for their first year away from home. There's no need to impress the opposite sex. You can wear whatever you want. This situation can be good for bonding with friends.

CONS: Nobody of the opposite sex.

. . . .

YOUR CALL

Some people loved it. Others not so much. Here are some things students had to say about living in a single-sex dorm.

> "Major girl cattiness. Total stereotype of gossip and backstabbing."

> "No girls in the dorm? Lame."

> "Really empowering. All the girls were so supportive of each other and we became really close."

> "Great, because I focused on studying and sleeping. I met girls in class, at night, so it didn't hurt my social life any."

. . . .

TWENTY-FOUR-HOUR QUIET HALLS

Some halls have noise restrictions—no loud parties or loud music allowed at any time.

PROS: It's easier to sleep and study without drunk people screaming up and down the halls and without loud music blasting from next door.

CONS: These quiet halls can have reputations as "dork dorms." This might or might not be true and students might or might not care. Some may find these dorms too quiet or antisocial.

From the outside, our dorm was the study dorm. I got the reaction "Ohhhh, you live in the HONORS dorm" from some people. But from the inside, people knew it was not as such. Some people had a full sound system that they would use at all hours of the night, and it would shake the walls and knock the plaster off! The girl across the hall from me was a sorority pledge who partied hard and came in at all hours of the night. So, I was living with some of the most intelligent people on campus I had ever met, but they also, despite what outside people might have thought, knew how to have fun.

—Sarah Mast, University of Southern California grad

LUXURY DORMS

The luxury hall is mainly a newer trend to attract students who want to live well, though some have been around for a while. These are otherwise known as "glam housing." The amenities can include:

- Spacious single or double rooms
- Private bathrooms
- Maid service
- Laundry service
- Beautiful views overlooking the water or city skylines
- Pools with sundecks, hot tubs
- Bathroom TVs
- Art and music studios
- Cafes, ultramodern gyms, and computer rooms

PROS: Hello? Just check out the amenities list!

CONS: These dorms can be *way* more expensive. They also might not allow freshmen or underclassmen. Luxury dorms may be considered too exclusive and sometimes have reputations as being snobby. You may have to enter a lottery to try to get a spot.

SUITES

Suites include several single or double rooms surrounding a common space and a bathroom shared only by the suite-mates. More and more schools are offering suite dorms.

· ·

WHERE'S YOUR DORM?

Your dorm location can have a surprisingly big impact on your daily routine. You don't always think about it before you move in, but when you compare notes with students on other parts of campus, you might realize that if your dorm is:

- near your classes, you can leave later or run back and get a book you forgot
- near the bars, you might be easily tempted to go out spontaneously and have people crash at your place
- near the library, you might use it to study more
- in another part of town or far away from the buildings you have classes in, you'll have to factor in commuting time
- near a parking lot, you'll have quicker access to your car, and if it's far away, you might go off campus less
- near a sports arena, you might be on the site of some tailgating
- near a shopping area, you might have to realllly watch your budget
- near a fraternity row, you'll have a shorter walk if you're pledging
- near a gym, it might make it more likely that you'll work out

· ·

PROS: Suites offer more bedroom privacy. It's nice to have a common area to hang out in, especially when guests come over. You're not sharing a bathroom with too many strangers. And if you don't bond with your room-mate, you might with a suitemate instead.

CONS: Not having to share a bathroom or television with forty other people can actually be isolating—you only have the chance to become really close to your suite-mates. There's also the possibility of disagreements over the common areas (i.e., who cleans them?).

> *The best thing about living in the dorms is the location,*
> *I think. If you're off campus, you're far away from things,*
> *even if you live right next door to the school. The dorms are*
> *sacred spaces where things happen that don't happen*
> *outside . . . there's more information there, more action,*
> *and more accommodations, like security, food,*
> *socialization . . .*
>
> —Joi, Emerson College (MA)

LIVING-LEARNING COMMUNITIES

If you want to connect with other students who have simi-lar interests, you may want to live in a living-learning com-munity or special-interest housing. These houses or halls focus on a certain theme or concept, linking some type of special interest or academic field to both in-class and out-of-class experiences. Faculty and staff often work directly with the students to support the themes. Classes geared toward the theme might be held in the hall. Tutoring and mentoring may be available. Be sure to ask when applying for residence if there are any theme halls available. Here are some examples:

- Many schools like Ohio University offer substance-free housing where residents sign a contract saying they'll abstain from alcohol or illegal drug use while living there.
- Students at Central Michigan University who are interested in campus leadership can live in the Leadership Hall.
- Schools like Texas Tech University and Rutgers University (NJ) offer special housing and support for students in recovery from alcohol and other drug addiction.
- Wesleyan University (CT) offers the first gender-free floor, where students aren't required to identify as male or female; the school welcomes both transgender and nontransgender individuals.
- Schools like the University of Maryland, College Park, have an International Hall where international students and students from the United States can live and learn together.
- The McLean Environmental Living and Learning Hall at Northland College (WI) is a "green" hall where students use wind generators, solar panels, and more to meet their environmentally friendly mission.
- Students at Cornell University (NY) can live in the Just About Music (JAM) dorm, which is for students with a passion for music, whether they be "an avid listener and lover of music, a shower singer, or those who have a more serious desire to become an accomplished musician."
- In Iowa, Cornell College's communities consist of a group of students with a common interest who live in a block of rooms together on campus. Their communities include service such as Kids Kare, which provides

care for the children of homeless single mothers, and Smiles for Seniors, in which students volunteer to work with the elderly.

- University of Minnesota students can live in the American Indian Cultural House if they're interested in past and contemporary American Indian issues and intercultural learning.

PROS: You'll learn more about your interests. You'll meet others with similar interests. And you might feel more comfortable from day one.

CONS: There will be less variety and less chance to meet people with different interests.

ROOMS

Face it, not all rooms are created equal. There's a huge variety in dorm room sizes, shapes, and how many people are stuffed into each one. And hey, most dorm rooms are small. Maybe smaller than the bedroom you grew up in. And you're sharing it with a stranger. Feeling claustrophobic? "Just think of the campus as your house. Your room is just where you are sleeping. Your living room is the lounge or the student center, your kitchen is the dining hall, the campus library is your study space," says George Brelsford, assistant vice president for Student Affairs and dean of students at Rowan University (NJ).

KINDS OF ROOMS

SINGLES: Yeah! Your own space! Privacy, nobody to fight with. Then again, nobody to bond with. Might be harder to find someone to hit the dining hall with you.

THE FIRST DORMS

The first residence halls at Oxford and Cambridge were built during the Middle Ages in the thirteenth century to fill the needs of students flocking to universities. (Many of them have both a dining hall and a small bar.) At the University of Paris, students camped in tents or burrowed themselves into the sides of the surrounding hills. In time they moved to live individually with schoolmasters or townspeople. Much later they started to rent big houses.

The first American dorms opened with the founding of nine colonial colleges—today's Ivy League universities. From the very beginning, they all had on-campus housing. Think your dorms are crazy?

- Fights, duels, and even murders were common in halls.
- Faculty and staff members were scared to death at the thought of being asked to go into a college dormitory.
- The halls were viewed by the public as places where one learns only bad manners.

Adapted from the website of Dr. Slobodan Box Zunic, adjunct professor of philosophy and hall director at the University of Rhode Island

DOUBLES: Another person to bond with. Then again, if you don't click, it's you versus them. You're stuck with this person, good or bad. (For now, anyway. More about dealing with a less-than-perfect roommate later.)

TRIPLES: Now you can bond with two people. Or, there can be two people to drive you crazy. If you're three stuffed into a small room, it's going to be crowded. And three's a crowd if two people bond and the other person is left out.

THE PRESIDENTIAL DORM?

"After exploring numerous avenues to meet the growing need [for student housing], we have offered to make our house available for housing 10-12 students," said the e-mail from Hannibal-LaGrange College's (MO) president, Woodrow Burt. He and his wife, English professor Katherine Burt, moved to temporary housing so twelve female students could still live on campus during their senior year.

—*The Chronicle of Higher Education,* August 13, 2004; the *Boston Globe* at boston.com, August 18, 2004; August 20, 2004

SUITES: Several students to bond with. But these rooms can also get cliquey if you only hang with people inside your suite. It can even get cliquey *inside* if some suitemates gang up on other ones.

PALACES AND DUNGEONS

Princeton Review publishes a list of college rankings, which includes lists of the best and the worst dorms. Here are the 2004 rankings:

DORMS LIKE PALACES

1. Pepperdine (CA)
2. Loyola College (MD)
3. Smith College (MA)
4. Scripps College (CA)
5. Bryn Mawr (PA)

DORMS LIKE DUNGEONS

1. University of Oregon
2. Florida A&M University
3. United States Coast Guard Academy (CT)
4. United States Merchant Marines (NY)
5. SUNY University at Albany (NY)

Students are able to immerse themselves in a total experience when they live on campus. They meet new people, study together, and make friends for life. They build a network that serves them well into their future. Many colleges and universities have or are creating living-learning environments where students and faculty from an area of specialty (or honors programs) live and work within the same residence hall. It is exceptional!

—Sallie Traxler, executive director of the Association of College and University Housing Officers–International

2

DORM, SWEET DORM

MOVE-IN DAY

It's move-in day in the dorms. The smell of cleaning products mingled with move-in sweat wafts up to greet you. The halls are colorful, covered with welcoming bulletin boards and doortags. There are people saying "Hey," hallways to navigate, and your room to find.

Welcome to your new home.

This is the time when students flood campus, lugging their belongings up to their rooms and settling in. It's exciting. It also can be confusing, crazy, and exhausting.

My first impressions: This lobby is huge. Which way do I go? Is that an RA? Ooh, cute. I hope he's my RA. Is the music always this loud? I hate this song. Okay, where's the elevator? That girl looks nice. That girl has a lot of piercings. Is the elevator always this slow? I'm so nervous to meet my roommate. Does the elevator always smell like this? I can't believe this is my new home!
—Kara, University of Michigan

WHEN TO ARRIVE

You may be tempted to arrive at the crack of dawn on move-in day. Okay, wait. Kory Vitangeli, the director of Residence Life at the University of Indianapolis (IN) suggests that you do not plan to arrive right when the residence halls open. You'll face long lines, traffic jams, and the most overanxious parents trying to move their kids in. Instead, wait three or four hours after the halls open. You'll still have plenty of time to get unpacked and prepare for the first activity. Plus, you'll have more personal assistance as the staff might have some downtime.

But if you do take this advice, remember that the last roommate in risks getting the last choice of bed. And closet. And dresser. And possibly wall space if your roommate(s) decorate quickly.

I mean, maybe you'll have considerate roommates who will wait for you. Like on some seasons of *The Real World,* where everyone wants to be fair and waits until all the roommates have arrived to pick beds and rooms. They talk about it or maybe pick randomly out of a hat. But more likely they won't wait for you. Like on other *Real World* seasons where the first person to get there claims a room and a bed right away and everyone else gets annoyed, but what can they do?

Just watch out. Because you could have written this in a letter to your new roommates over the summer: "Hi! I'm Julia! I'm really easy to live with and have no requests except that I am really not good at sleeping on the top bunk, as I found out in camp when I rolled off and hurt myself. So I will trade anything if you let me avoid the top bunk. Thanks." And then you end up being the last roommate to arrive and find out that the other two have ignored your ONLY request and have left you the top bunk, anyway. And they're like, "Sorry, you were the last one here, and we're not switching."

Oooookay. And yes, I did fall off the bed. A lot.

EARLY ARRIVAL REQUEST

If you absolutely think you *must* arrive early for any reason, check with the Housing office first to see what their policy is on early arrival. Some halls charge for early arrival. Other times you need to have a valid reason to move in early. Residence hall staff don't have much time to get the rooms ready for occupancy, and early arrivals can often make it hard for them to get everything done. Basically this can be a huge hassle for everyone involved, so make sure you really need to do it, and ask early!

THE MOVE-IN CREW

Many schools provide moving assistance for students and their families. Some offer more help than others. Some schools have orientation staff available to point you in the right direction or to help in a crisis, but not to help actually move you. University of Arizona posts "Ask Me" volunteers at various locations around campus to provide answers to your questions and to provide students with a "smiling, helpful face." Other schools offer more. Penn State (PA) calls their moving crew the "Hall Haulers." These students from campus organizations and the orientation staff volunteer to help new students unload their cars and carry their belongings up to their rooms.

No one will do all of the moving for you, though, unless you've hired them yourself. You'll need to be actively involved in the unloading process, especially since you'll be able to pull your car up in front of the dorm for only a short time, or possibly not at all.

Follow the directions provided by your campus Housing office and stick to the move-in day process to ensure that move-in goes smoothly. Some campuses give specific information online, so check your college website for the latest information.

Ready to move?

- *Don't expect access to an elevator.* There may be some running, but chances are, they'll be crowded. Be prepared to use the stairs at some point, especially if you live on a lower floor.

- *Bring your own cart.* There are usually some moving carts available for students to use, but if you want to make it easy on yourself, consider bringing your own dolly so you won't have to wait for one to become available.

- *Consider shipping some things.* This might be an easier way to get some things to school, especially if you live far away. If you're taking a plane, bus, or train, you'll be limited to several bags. Check your school's policy on storing shipped items, though, before you take this step. You might need to have your parents send it along after you've already moved in.

- *Pack a small cooler.* You'll want to have something cool and refreshing to quench your thirst. Soda machines usually empty fast!

Contributions from Alison Cummings, assistant director of Residence Life at Penn State University (PA); and Lakecia Johnson-Harris, assistant director of Residence Life at the University of Southern Mississippi

You might consider getting a moving kit. Dorm-room kits at office supply stores can include boxes of different sizes, bubble wrap, tape, markers, computer-protection kits, and mailing supplies such as tubes.

PARENTS OR NO PARENTS?

Some students are on their own moving into the dorms. They might choose to do it themselves so they can start independence right away. Or, their parents may live far away, or family circumstances may not work out for parents to come along.

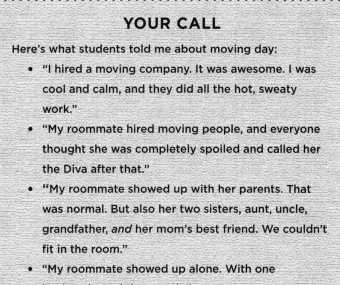

YOUR CALL

Here's what students told me about moving day:

- "I hired a moving company. It was awesome. I was cool and calm, and they did all the hot, sweaty work."
- "My roommate hired moving people, and everyone thought she was completely spoiled and called her the Diva after that."
- "My roommate showed up with her parents. That was normal. But also her two sisters, aunt, uncle, grandfather, *and* her mom's best friend. We couldn't fit in the room."
- "My roommate showed up alone. With one backpack. And that was it."

Many parents are there on move-in day. They want to make sure you've got everything you need, they also want to check out your roommate, and it's their last chance to say good-bye before their baby goes off on their own. You might be happy to have them there—or have no choice if your parents insist—helping you set up, decorate, and unpack. Plus, they might buy you lunch and new stuff for your room if they see you need it.

For students whose families come, good-byes can be short and sweet. Or they can drag on. And on. Alison at Penn State says, "Although it's hard to say good-bye, the family and significant others who are still around as you're settling in can hinder your ability to connect with the new people on your floor." She suggests that families do their final farewell dinner at home before getting to campus because there may not be time to do it once you arrive. "Most first-year students I see are wanting to jump into activities," Alison says, "but they can feel a little pulled when their families stick around."

Susan Ratz-Thomas, the assistant dean of Student Life and coordinator of Judicial Affairs at Southern Methodist University (TX), agrees: "It's probably not a good idea for parents to stay for two to three days," she says, recalling one family at a former institution who parked their RV in a campus parking lot and stayed for days after moving their student into the dorm. "Those conversations need to happen *before* you get to campus—where you talk about at what point Mom and Dad are going to leave."

It can be comfortable having your parents in the dorm, or it might be way uncomfortable. Your parents might embarrass you. They can make a big fuss. They can be too chatty and ask prying questions and scare off your roommates. They can treat you like a baby. They can be too conspicuous. Or maybe you're just worried that people will think you're just like them—and you're so not.

But even though the day is all about you, take a minute and remember it's a big deal for them, too. So ease them out with some care. Hug them, kiss them, and remember their feelings. If you want them to leave, tell them you need some alone time to get used to your new situation. Make a plan to call them or e-mail them soon. Tell them something nice and heartfelt that they can think of fondly during their trip back home. It can be really emotional for parents to say their final good-byes. So be gentle when you kick them out the door. Maybe *nudge* them out instead.

WHAT TO BRING

It can be easy to throw everything that holds any meaning to you in a box. But then you'd need to rent out three extra rooms, just to hold your stuff. Pare it down to just essentials. And remember, if you have a roommate, you will most likely get his or her phone number or e-mail address at some point during the summer. Contact him or her to coordinate what each of you is bringing so you don't have duplicates of things you only need one of. If there is extra stuff you both want, you should figure out who's going to buy it (and what the budget is) or if you're going to wait and get it together once you move in. You should also coordinate decorating ideas!

HERE'S WHAT TO BRING . . . OR PLAN TO GET ASAP

1. Items you and your roommates will need only one of

   - Memo board for door
   - TV
   - CD player
   - Area rug
   - Window coverings (curtains—your window will most likely have blinds)
   - Mirror
   - Room phone
   - Microwave (sometimes provided)
   - Minifridge (sometimes provided)
   - Answering machine
   - Fan, if you don't have AC
   - Beanbag chair

2. Items that serve double duty or save space
   - Trunks can serve as coffee tables
   - Large pillows are great for reading in bed and for creating extra seating
   - Plastic crates
   - Underbed storage units (make sure there's space under your bed before buying them)
   - Yaffa blocks
   - Over-door pocket storage hangers or shoe hangers
   - Rolling plastic drawers

3. Appliances and technology
   - Laptop or desktop computer
   - Printer
   - Cell phone
   - iPod, Walkman with headphones
   - Alarm clock
   - Calculator
   - Lamp
   - Camera
   - Extension cord
   - Iron

4. Hobbies/recreational equipment
   - Exercise mat
   - Bike
   - Tennis racket
   - Sneakers
   - Musical instrument

- Frisbee, football, etc.
- Bathing suit

5. Personal items
   - Medication
   - Address/phone book with important numbers
   - Insurance information
   - Photos and photo albums
   - Plastic bucket to carry toiletries to shared bathroom
   - Toothbrush/toothpaste
   - Hair-care products
   - Hairdryer
   - Deodorant
   - Makeup and perfume
   - Shaving stuff
   - Laundry detergent
   - Laundry bag or basket
   - Towels
   - Flip-flops to wear to shower, especially if you share with more than a few people
   - Bottle opener
   - Hangers

6. Cleaning supplies
   - Dust cloths
   - Disinfectant wipes
   - A whisk broom and dustpan
   - Toolkit, or at least a hammer and screwdriver

7. Bedding

- Sheets to fit—sometimes you'll need extra-long ones
- Comforter
- Pillows and pillowcases
- Extra blanket for bed and to drag out to TV lounge

8. School supplies

- Pens
- Stapler
- Scissors
- Computer paper
- Notebooks
- Highlighters
- Folders
- Poster-hanging supplies
- Paper clips

Contributions by Denise Marcoux Nelson, the director of Residential Life at the University of Southern Maine

Also remember to check out your college's website or student newspaper for specific tips. Here are some examples.

Smith College (MA) recommends:
A heavy coat, gloves, a hat, a scarf, and warm, water-proof boots for our Massachusetts winters, which can come in November and stay until March. Boots and shoes with good traction are a big help on icy days. For rain, you'll need a slicker and a rain hat or umbrella.

The University of Southern Florida recommends:

Shorts, T-shirts, walking shoes are all necessities. Leave the winter-woolies behind. You'd only use them for a short time in January and February.

Yale's (CT) **Daily News** *recommends:*

Bring some semiformal attire because there are a few freshmen orientation events that require you to dress up. You will also want formal attire—nice shoes and your old prom dress or a tux—for such galas as Casino Night and the Winter Ball.

The University of North Dakota site says:

While there will be a dance before Fall Break, bring any dresses you may want, but don't feel like you have to have a dress . . . there are always plenty of people around to borrow from.

Stanford University (CA) recommends:

We offer a delivery service for basic supplies. Order items like detergents, bed linens, cookware, and towels, and they'll arrive in your dorm room the next day!

WHAT *NOT* TO BRING

You will most likely have to focus on weeding some stuff out.

No matter where you go to school, you cannot take everything from your room at home and bring it to campus. Why? One reason is because your roommate will be trying to bring everything from his or her room at home to campus. If it won't fit in the backseat and trunk of the car, then you're bringing too much stuff.

Remember, you're going to college, not the Gulag.
Sometime before you get your degree, you'll go home to
visit, so you'll have plenty of opportunity to bring more
stuff if you need it. And the postal service does deliver
to most campuses, as does UPS. Using them will not
only keep the economy going, it'll save your father's back
on move-in day.

>   —Jim Carley, the associate director of Residential Life at
>   Keene State College (NH)

Lyn Redington, associate director of Residence, and
Drake Martin, assistant director of Residence at the University of Northern Iowa, warn against bringing the following to school:

- Candles (most dorms don't allow them)
- Drum sets (even if they were allowed, you *don't* want to be that person!)
- Air conditioners (provided or prohibited)
- Irreplaceable valuables (duh)
- Pets (except fish, if allowed)
- Hanging items that need nails (bring sticky hanging putty for posters)
- Hot plates (things with open flames or coils)
- Explosives (fireworks, etc.)
- Halogen lightbulbs (fire hazard)
- Illegal drugs (duh)
- Incense (not a great idea)
- Vacuum cleaner (often provided in each house)
- Waterbed (your bed will most likely be provided)
- Weapons (prohibited)

ROOM STUFF

This year, college students are expected to spend an average of $605.69 of their own money on stuff for college, according to a survey conducted by BIGresearch for the National Retail Federation. More and more stores are targeting college student needs with special "Dorm Designs." These items can make your room funky, organized, efficient, and less blah. Some of the following sites and stores even have registries, so set yourself up for graduation or back-to-school presents.

- The Container Store at www.thecontainerstore.com
- Target, including the Todd Oldham line, at stores and target.com
- Linens-n-Things has a Destination Dorm campaign
- Bed Bath & Beyond has a bedbathandbeyond.com college registry
- PBteen has a college dorm checklist
- AllDorm.com
- IKEA stores and IKEA.com
- Collegiatemall.com
- StudentMarket.com
- Dormworld.com
- Staples and staples.com

If you're bringing stuff in more than one vehicle, you are bringing too much stuff. I once stopped a car that was fully loaded and asked the driver what building they were moving into. "Oh! I don't know. Ask my daughter;

she's in the next car." I went to the next car—also
fully loaded—and asked that driver the same question.
"Um . . . I'm not sure. Ask my sister; she's in the next
car." So I went to the third car—loaded as well—and
finally got the answer I needed. As I turned to go, she
said, "Could you tell the guys in the next car where we're
going? I don't think they know."

—Jim Carley, the associate director of Residential Life at
Keene State College (NH)

PETS

One of the hardest rules to abide by is the No Pets Allowed
policy that is enforced in most residence halls. Why can't
you have a cute little kitten or a bunny? Well, think about
it for a minute. A dorm room really doesn't have a whole
lot of space for an animal. They'd probably go stir crazy,
and their quality of life would just suck. Plus, so many students just dump their illegal kittens or dogs at the end of
the year because they can't take them home. You know
what often happens in those scenarios . . . really sad.

A very few college dorms actually allow dogs and cats.
SUNY Canton in New York allows certain pets in one pet-
friendly hall. Stephens College in Missouri has started allowing several students to have dogs, cats, and rabbits in
some rooms. And there are many dorms that do allow you
to have certain kinds of smaller pets. Check with your RA to
see if fish or hamsters are allowed. Just remember, if you do
keep a pet, make sure you're committed to it year-round.
The pet doesn't stop needing to eat or have its cage
cleaned just because you have finals or summer break.

Two women had a large fish tank in their room. They had
a friend of theirs look after the fish when they were away

for spring break. Well, I think the friend got the "heater knob" confused with a different knob, because at the end of the break, we all came back and the entire hallway smelled like boiled fish! It was awful.

—Penny Pasque, research assistant at the University of
    Michigan's National Forum on Higher Education for the
    Public Good

YOUR CAR

First, check to see if you're allowed to have cars at school. At some schools, freshmen in particular face restrictions. Before you leave for school, find out where to park and how to pay for parking. And be sure your car is serviced and that your insurance information and owner's manual are in the glove box, along with a flashlight.

Be prepared: You should keep a basic emergency kit in your trunk and have a local map handy. Have at least one extra set of keys in a safe place, such as your room or with Public Safety, in case you lose yours.

Once you get to school, follow the same driving rules you had banged into your head when you got your license. Don't drink and drive. Don't let anyone else drive your car. And follow school regulations like not parking in the professor's spot when you're late to class. That's a hard one, but getting tickets means you're going to owe a lot of money. And getting towed? It sucks.

I went to Ohio State for grad school. It was my first day on campus, and I swear I didn't see the NO PARKING sign. My car got towed. Nice—and expensive—welcome to my new school! But it did make me verrry careful where I parked for the next three years.

Appreciate people who have cars. Some campuses have

a lot of students with cars, and it's no big deal. At others, though, it's a prized commodity to get off campus. If you share rides, offer to share gas expenses at least.

- -

TOP TEN THINGS YOU WANT IN YOUR DORM ROOM

10. Posters

9. Black light

8. VCR/TiVo system

7. DVD player

6. TV

5. Stuffed animal (to show your softer side)

4. Refrigerator

3. Christmas lights

2. Telephone

1. Computer

TOP FIVE THINGS YOU *DON'T* WANT IN YOUR DORM ROOM

5. Molding food

4. Annoying roommates

3. Dirty boys

2. Computer viruses

1. Little sisters

—Harmony, student at Temple University (PA)

- -

PHONE SERVICE

One decision you'll have to make is whether to have phone service installed in your room. As soon as you get your address and dorm-room assignment, you'll be able to do that. Your school will provide instructions on how to set it up. You might have to call the phone company and arrange to have it activated. Check out the different plans to find the best rates for monthly fees and long distance.

If you're sharing phone service with a roommate, set it up in everyone's names—if it's just in your name and your roommate skips out, you're stuck with the bill. Each roommate should have his own PIN code for long distance. Don't give this code out to anyone or you'll get stuck with any abuse that occurs. Some schools, like Dartmouth (NH), are creating systems where students can get phone service via computer instead of a regular phone. Expect this to become a trend in coming years.

Cell phones are rapidly becoming a major way to communicate on campus. It's estimated that about three out of four students bring cell phones with them to college. Check to see if your school offers deals on cell phone rates. Many schools are negotiating service plans to meet student demand and possibly make some money for the college itself.

3

A ROOM OF YOUR OWN (SORT OF)

IT'S YOURS

Your room. That has a really nice ring to it, eh? This cozy little cubicle (or part of one) may not seem like much at first, but it's *your* space.

If you took a campus tour, you probably saw a sample dorm room. Guess what? It might look nothing like yours. "If you've done a campus tour and seen a room," warns Alison Cummings, assistant director of Residence Life at Penn State University, "that may not necessarily be the kind of room you get." If you're nearby and want to check out your room beforehand, some colleges will let you look at it before move-in day. Other colleges offer room information and dimensions on their campus website. Like if you're moving into Bryn Mawr's (PA) Erdman Room 101, you can learn online that the desk has four drawers and that in the afternoon the windows face the sun . . . and that the room is shaped like Nevada! And virtual tours online can give you a good 360-degree view.

I have to admit I freaked when I saw my dorm room. I felt claustrophobic when I realized I [was] really going to be living here. With other human beings I never knew or heard of. In my bedroom. Just yesterday my mom wouldn't let me have strange people sleep in my bedroom.

—Jen, University of Vermont

Just so there's no confusion, Alison suggests that if you're planning to bring large items (lofts, furniture, etc.), contact the Residence Life office ahead of time—you don't want your parents to have to bring something "labor intensive" back home. "Make sure that what you're bringing is allowed and will fit," Alison says.

If you're way organized, you might ask about:

- The size of your dorm room—complete with all measurements. You might need this for buying carpets or rugs
- The number and measurements of the windows
- The built-in storage space
- Furniture—is there more than just the basics (bed, dresser, and desk)?
- The lighting or lamps that come with the room
- The number of outlets

Before you come to college, picture every dorm room you've seen on television or in the movies. Now, picture one about a quarter the size and without the trendy furniture. That is what you'll be living in.

—Matthew Herek, Residence director at DePaul
  University (IL)

YOUR NEW SPACE

First, this space is yours for the taking. Set up a few of your favorite things right away to make it feel like home, whether it's pictures, plants, or fuzzy pillows on your bed.

Also keep in mind that this new room won't be looking like your old room back home. For one thing, you're sharing it with a person you may never have met and who has tastes and favorite items, too. For another, it's a *new* space—a place to assert your new beginning. Do you want it to look *exactly* like the room you left behind? Nah. Time to start fresh.

The walls will be a neutral, possibly ugly, color (probably white). The furniture will be a neutral, possibly ugly, color (probably beige). You'll think you walked into Blahville. But, hey, once you and your roommate(s) enter, there will be LIFE in the room! And that, plus a few posters, can add a whole world of color.

What you can't do much about is the squish factor. Dorm rooms are notoriously small. They're not necessarily the sardine cans they're made out to be, but they're not Trump Tower, either. A little bit of planning and prioritizing can help you maximize your space, even if it is space-challenged.

It's your choice. You can make it feel like a home you can truly live in, or you can decide to just deal. If you hate it, well, you'll move sometime. It's temporary. There's no twenty-four-year-old college graduate still living in a dorm room.

Making the most of your minidomain is all in the setup. Not sure what you want to do? Consider checking out what other students have done. There's always the famous "You should see what they've done!" room. That doesn't mean you should copy their ideas, but it might serve as inspiration.

BEDS

You'll have to get used to a new bed. Be ready for the Goldilocks syndrome—beds that are harder, softer, shorter, longer than you're used to. If your bed is really uncomfortable, consider buying a feather bed for the top of it—the extra fluff might help. A body pillow or a foam microbed thing might help, too.

BUNKING OR LOFTING

Consider bunking your beds so they're not taking up so much surface area; if the beds aren't bunkable, consider lofting them with a wooden bunk-bed setup (which you'll probably have to build yourself). Find out what your school does when it comes to lofts: Do you have to buy special kits directly from the institution, do you have to use special woods if you make your own, is the pre-existing furniture in the room loftable? Ask the questions before you get started. You can usually have the beds traditionally bunked or with the bed underneath sticking out perpendicularly, or you can loft your beds with desk space underneath. Talk with your roommate first and decide together how to handle who will sleep where. Maybe one of you loves the top bunk—dilemma solved! Or maybe you can switch off every other month. Come to some resolution that's comfortable for both of you, and if you can't, forget the whole bunk-bed deal! It's not worth causing tumult. Just remember to ask before you move in if the beds are bunkable and if maintenance has special attachments that need to be put in place to make your bunks safe and sound.

ATTACHED BEDS

Some beds are attached to desks. Don't try to dismantle these pieces on your own. If you do, you'll likely get injured somehow, or you'll break something and be charged for damages. Talk with your RA and maintenance staff.

FUTON

A futon is a Japanese-style mattress placed on the floor or on a folding wooden frame. Some futons can be folded into couches and then unfolded into a bed. If your dorm room is unfurnished and you want to have a couch, a futon might be a good space-saver to consider.

SHEETS

Do the beds in your dorm take extra-long, extra-short, or regular-size sheets? That simple question can make all the difference between a nice, neat, tucked-in bed and a rumpled, rustled mess.

> *If you have the chance, take the top bunk because when you have a party in your room, usually people won't go onto your bed unless you invite them up.*
>
> —Joe Bartozzi, resident assistant at Western Connecticut State University

CLOSETRY

Dorm closets aren't known for spaciousness, either. You might have your own closet, or you might have to split it with a roomie. Here are some tips on how to maximize your closet space:

- *Use shelves wisely.* Top shelves can be out of reach. Make it easier to pull things down by putting a few bins or laundry baskets up there so you don't have individual items crashing down on you. Then, store things you don't need every day, like extra shampoo and school supplies, in the baskets.
- *Make a closet door.* Some closets are wide open. If your closet doesn't have a door and you want to hide your clutter, a shower curtain can do the trick.
- *Put your dresser in there.* Many students opt to put their dresser in their closet (if it fits) to keep the room organized and to free up more floor space. Check to see if

there are any policies against this type of move before doing it, though.

—Jeff Kegolis, former assistant director of Residence Life and current assistant professor of psychology at King's College (PA)

STORAGE STATIONS

- *Find out about storage options ahead of time.* Don't assume that your dorm will have space for you to store boxes, luggage, and other hard-to-fit items. Many of them just don't have the space. Call ahead or ask questions at orientation to find out what's possible. Colleges may offer extra storage, but you need to check on availability and pricing. For example, your dorm might offer trunk space for luggage or furniture storage for students living abroad for a semester.
- *Under the bed.* Some schools let you raise your bed up on special risers so there's more space for storage underneath. Get a few underbed storage containers that slide easily in and out, and use them to store stuff like extra sheets and towels.
- *Bring stackable luggage.* If possible, bring luggage that lets you store one inside another. It'll be easier to tuck away in your closet or under your bed. Or, use your luggage itself as storage space.

IS THIS LEGAL?
Before you get to campus and realize that half your belongings are against school policy, it's best to check ahead by

- asking questions at orientation;
- calling up the Residence Life or the Housing office;
- reading the student handbook online;
- Going over that room-and-board contract you signed.

Many Residence Life or Housing offices also put out print and online publications about what you can and can't bring.

INSIDER TIPS

- Ask for the Housing office's policies on nails and on moving in extra furniture.

- Make sure any furnishings you provide are flame-resistant.

- Painting or wallpaper probably won't be permitted, but it never hurts to ask.

- Most loft designs have to be approved in advance of construction.

- Most older halls have a limit to the electrical capacity for each room.

Contributed by Lakecia Johnson-Harris, assistant director of Residence Life at the University of Southern Mississippi

AVOIDING ROOM DAMAGE

When you're setting up your room, you're probably not thinking about room damage. You just want to get things situated so you can dive into the semester and have a comfortable place to come home to. But to save yourself money and hassle at the end of the year when you're checking out of your room, keep a few "room damage preventers" in mind:

- Don't use duct tape to keep your carpet in place—it creates an icky, gooey mess when you pull that carpet up, and you'll likely be charged for floor cleaning.

- Don't use spray snow on your windows or mirrors—it often stains, believe it or not, and can be impossible to remove.

- Don't put glow-in-the-dark stars on your ceiling—some schools will charge you for each star left behind, which can get way costly.
- Don't leave spills unattended. Clean up the cranberry juice in the fridge, the shampoo that fell behind your dresser, and the pen that exploded in your desk drawer now! Spills that are left for months tend to leave permanent stains, which you'll be charged for.
- Don't have a dartboard behind your door or on your wall—the number of dart holes you'll have to pay for is definitely NOT worth it.
- Don't nail things into the wall—removing the nails can leave *chunks* in the plaster, making nail holes thirty times their original size.

You'll sign a room-condition report of some kind when you move in. Fill it out thoroughly, marking down any preexisting damage; then make sure the room is in the same shape when you move out. You have better things to do with your money than to pay damage bills.

Worried about masking tape pulling the paint off those freshly painted residence hall walls? Consider using painter's tape, like they do at the University of California, Davis. All RAs are provided with rolls of the substance for posting flyers and other necessary "stuff" in their hallways. Check with your dorm staff first to see if it's okay to use painter's tape in your room to hang up your posters. It'll help you avoid end-of-the-year charges for tape marks on the walls!

—Stephanie Hubbard, assistant director of Student Housing at UC Davis

TECHNOLOGY

Technology plays a huge role in college students' lives. In most modern dorm rooms, you can find a TV, VCR, DVD player, portable CD players, cell phones, digital cameras, computers and all the stuff that comes with them, and much more.

Most students bring the technology themselves. However, more and more campuses are offering technology free to their students. Some lucky college students are now receiving cell phones, BlackBerries, iPods, USB key-chain storage devices, and computers. Plus, more and more campuses are offering downloadable music services so students don't do it illegally, so check with your campus policies.

Dell, Yahoo!, and Google were all started in college dorms.

COMPUTERS

Some colleges are more wired than others. Some loan out laptops to students for a semester. Others rent out laptops or desktops. And there are always computer labs for students who don't have their own computers or who need certain capabilities theirs don't have.

Do some research before buying a computer for your dorm room. You'll want to see what your college offers, allows, and is best set up for. Some Admissions offices, like the one at the University of Minnesota, Duluth, list computer specifics so students know what tech tools they need to bring to campus.

Here are some factors to consider:

- *Cost.* Compare prices. Many colleges participate in discount programs with major manufacturers.
- *Software.* Find out whether the college offers free or reduced-price software.
- *Maintenance.* Is there a warranty? Don't forget availability and cost of repair services.
- *Campus recommendations.* For students buying new computers, colleges often recommend getting a fast one with a big hard drive.
- *Storage space.* Some schools also suggest extra features, such as a CD burner to save or back up data. Students should check whether their campus network provides storage space, so they can access information from home or from a lab without carrying a disk.
- *Networks.* Student computers need to have the right cards installed to access campus networks. Some schools specify a certain type of Ethernet card to connect to the Internet from dorm rooms. Some schools also have wireless technology on parts of the campus, making it possible to access the Internet from a variety of locations from a laptop. Your dorm will provide you with this information.
- *Accessories.* For printers and other accessories, check what student printing and other facilities are available at the college, and check their cost and accessibility.

Adapted from "Buying a Computer Is Just One More Decision to Make," February 26, 2002, Eleanor Chute, Pittsburgh *Post-Gazette*

LAPTOPS VS. DESKTOP COMPUTERS

What's best for campus? A portable laptop, or a nice big PC with all the trimmings? Consider the pros and cons:

- You can take a laptop outside, to class, or to the library. You'd look funny doing that with a desktop—plus you'd need a really long extension cord.
- It's much easier for someone to walk off with your laptop than a desktop.
- When you have a computer problem, it's easier to carry a laptop to a computer technician.
- If you have a desktop, your roommate or room visitors might be inclined to use it because it's sitting right there. You can put a laptop away—out of sight, out of mind.
- If you need to type a paper late at night, a laptop lets you do that somewhere else so you're not keeping your roommate awake with "tap-a-tap-tap."
- Desktops typically have bigger screens so your eyes don't go as buggy.
- Laptops can be damaged more easily (they get overheated more quickly, they can be dropped, etc.).

Many campuses have an Operation ID or some other engraving program, typically available through Public Safety or Security. Whether you have a laptop or a desktop, it's a good idea to get your valuables—including computers—engraved with your driver's license or some other number (not your social security number!) that you can then put on file with Public Safety. This makes it much easier to track stolen stuff.

E-MAIL ADDRESS

Typically, when you go to orientation or when you move in, you'll get all the details about how to sign up for a school e-mail address. Ask if this address will be good during the summers, too, when you may not be on campus. Also ask how long it will work after you graduate. Lots of schools give you an alumni e-mail address once you graduate, too!

SETTING UP YOUR COMPUTER SPACE

When you set up your computer or clear a space for your laptop, keep the following ergonomic considerations in mind so you don't harm yourself:

SEE STRAIGHT. Adjust the computer monitor height so that the screen's top is at or slightly below eye level. Your eyes should look slightly downward when viewing the middle of the screen.

AVOID MUSCLE FATIGUE. Steer clear of long periods of repetitive activity. Alternate activities.

PROTECT THOSE WRISTS. If you look at the anatomy of the wrist, it is curved away from any contact surface. Try to follow that natural curve as you place your mouse.

REST YOUR ARMS. Use armrests, because they reduce the effects of carpal tunnel syndrome and even help prevent developing it. Make sure that keyboards are low, at about wrist height, to reduce the angle of the wrists.

Contributed by Andrea Borean, a graduate of Rowan University (NJ)

COMPUTER HELP

Most campuses have Help Desks and/or ResNet folks (dedicated solely to the residential computer network in the residence halls) whom you can call with computer questions. Some colleges even have trained students or professionals who will come to your room to help with computer issues. You'll typically have to make an appointment with them, so don't always expect immediate results. Be safe and back up your work on disk all the time so you don't run into a real emergency.

An important computer reminder: Be in tune with campus computer warnings about worms, viruses, and more. Most campuses will give you access to instructions, software, security patches, and other tools to clean your system right away. Do it!!

BLOGS, WEBCAMS, AND MORE

Want to find out more about what other college students are doing on campus? Want to share your life with others? Student weblogs (blogs) are one way to do it. Some colleges even showcase student blogs to prospective students to show them what campus life is like. Simmons College (MA), for example, includes five blogs from freshmen on its site. Here are excerpts from a couple of them:

Katherine's student blog says, "The two girls across the hall aren't getting along anymore. So Susan is moving in with me, and Jill is moving in with Meredith. I will miss Jill. She was a good roommate. We didn't really hang out as friends, but we were good as roommates. We're just really easy-going. I hope rooming with Susan will be the same way."

And Justine says: "We usually spend the evenings popping into each others' rooms and using what little time there is to do homework for a much more entertaining purpose: hall bonding. In fact, around 9:00 P.M. is the busiest time in the hall because everyone is finally coming home from their long day."

IPODS: THE NEXT COLLEGE MUST-HAVE?

We know they're for music. And for college students? Duke University (NC) thinks they're so valuable, they distributed iPods for free. They say students will use them as minicomputers for educational uses, such as listening to lectures, practicing foreign languages, and studying dialects.

"There's nothing the student can do with an iPod that he couldn't do with a laptop," says Duke vice president Tracy Futhey. "But the mobility and power in that small package means they'll most likely take it with them everywhere."

Apple vice president Greg Joswiak predicts many other schools will follow suit. Duke is creating a special website for students that will offer downloads of lessons and sales of digital music.

—"Duke Passes Out iPods for Educational Use," Jefferson Graham, *USA Today,* July 20, 2004

Other blogs are entirely non-campus affiliated—just students posting their own stuff online. Sometimes it's TMI. But, it's one way to find out about different personalities who live on campuses.

And webcams . . . well, they totally vary. For example:

. . . .

TOP TEN WAYS TO KEEP TECHNOLOGY FROM OVERWHELMING YOUR LIFE

It can be easy to set up your room like an isolation booth as you take some classes online, communicate with people electronically, and eat takeout food from the dining hall while sitting at your desk. Technology can be a positive and a negative. Avoid the negatives.

10. Remember to take study and computer breaks. It helps to get a few minutes away from the computer screen or from books, even when a big project is due.

9. Don't count forty-five minutes of IMs and fifteen minutes of Internet research as an hour of study time. Sometimes you just need to turn the instant messenger and the cell phone off to get work done.

8. The best way to communicate with your roommate is not through e-mail.

7. If the only smile people ever see from you is :) , you might want to get away from the computer more.

6. Sometimes the best part of watching a movie or TV show is sharing it with others. Watch the big game or the afternoon soap opera in the TV lounge or invite some friends over to watch it.

5. If it will take you the same amount of time to go down the hall to ask a neighbor a question as it would take to ring them on their cell, get the exercise!

4. Too much of anything is usually not a good thing, and that includes technology.

3. Learn a few lessons on cell phone and e-mail etiquette, and share these lessons with others.

2. Just because you can take your laptop or PDA everywhere, doesn't mean you should.

1. Realize that your college years will not be remembered for getting the high score on a video game or for your witty e-mail jokes; they will be remembered for the friendships that you make.

—Aaron F. Lucier, the assistant director for technology and assignments in East Carolina University's (NC) Campus Living department

- The University of Colorado at Boulder's webcam shows scenes around the campus, including a Rocky Mountain view.
- Cornell's (NY) webcam shows students making SEND MONEY signs with their bodies.
- Penn State's webcam features their football stadium cam.
- Appalachian State's (NC) webcam shows their parking lot cam.

And of course, some students have their own webcams live from their dorm rooms. Some are pretty tame. Others . . . not. Some exist to charge you money, so be warned.

Other online services that campus residents are using include the facebook.com, a website that features photos and short bios of students on some campuses used for networking and making friends. Some colleges and their students run online dating services that can help connect you with fellow students.

· ·

NEVER WOULD HAVE
THOUGHT ABOUT IT BUT . . .

"Electrical use is still at a premium on most college campuses. Therefore, more and more schools are encouraging and even mandating the use of low-wattage appliances." So . . .

- look for the ENERGY STAR label on appliances.
- microfridges take up less space and use less energy than a separate microwave and refrigerator.
- power strips with built-in surge protectors are essential.
- additional lighting (clip-on lights, floor lamps, desk lamps, etc.) is generally needed to supplement existing overhead lighting, but it's best to check out what is permitted.

—Denise Marcoux Nelson, the director of Residential Life at the University of Southern Maine

· ·

DORM DECORATING 101

Okay, now comes the fun stuff. According to a National Retail Federation survey, parents and students will spend $2.6 billion each year just on dorm and apartment furnishings. You can choose to purchase that same hot movie star poster or *Starry Night* print by Van Gogh that everyone has, or you can make an individual statement all your own.

THE ROOM MESSAGE CHECK

Personalizing your space is important. You want your dorm room to feel comfortable to you and, of course, to your roommate(s). Another factor to consider is making your room welcoming to *others*. (At least if you're hoping to have some friends over.)

- -

TOP POSTER TYPES FOUND IN DORM ROOMS—UNSCIENTIFIC SURVEY

- Music
- Movies
- Celebrities
- Art
- Hot models
- Animals
- Motivation
- Party posters
- Cartoon
- Sports

What statement do you want to make?

- -

Some students want just the basics: a couple posters and a few colorful storage bins. That's the norm in many halls. Putting nothing on the walls also makes a statement: I don't really care. Easy? Yeah, but boring and kind of freaky to have *nothing* in there. Other students go all out. More ideas for that later.

Whether you're into NASCAR or the National Ballet, your room reflects your passions and interests. It also sends messages about who you are and what you believe, whether you intend it to or not. That's why stepping back and doing a dorm-room "message check" can help you see your room through other people's eyes:

- *Look at the outside of your room door.* What does it communicate? What could people think about your personality based on the jokes/comics you have posted? What does your message board say? If someone were to pass by, would they feel welcomed by your door decorations?

- *What's on your walls?* Your choice of posters and pictures tells a lot about you. People will immediately make assumptions about who you are by what you hang. Check if you're making the impression you want: Is there anything offensive on your walls that could make someone of a different gender, sexual orientation, race, or ability feel unwelcome in your room?

YOUR CALL

"Our dorm goes crazy on our rooms, and we love it. Practically everyone has a theme."

"Some people go way overboard. Huge decorating budgets. Matching designer everything or fantasy theme rooms. In our dorm it's totally trying too hard."

"Some of the people in our hall are *Trading Spaces* fans. So we all redid each others' rooms on a budget."

"Decorating? I just stuck with the two Cs: cheap and comfortable."

THEME ROOMS

Theme rooms are based on your interests, personality, or just crazy ideas. Of course, you'll need to have your room-mate(s) in on this. Themes might be:

- Bohemian
- Sports
- School spirit
- Greek
- Artsy
- Surfer
- Musical
- Retro decades: '60s, '70s, '80s
- Patriotic
- Safari
- Moon and stars
- Nature
- Hobbies
- Urban
- Animals
- Disco
- Movies

SEATING

You'll want to have enough room for you and your guests to sit and hang out—other than on the bed. For example:

- Beanbag chairs
- Butterfly chairs
- Ottomans (some even have extra storage inside)
- Floor pillows

- Futons (some convert from couch to bed if you've got the space)
- Gaming rockers
- Inflatable chairs
- Hammocks

BUDGET DORM ROOMS

It's not necessary to spend a lot of money on your dorm room. If you're on a budget, go check out:

- thrift and secondhand stores
- garage sales and tag sales
- outlet malls
- IKEA
- flea markets
- dollar stores
- eBay

Or try to get crafty and DIY:

- Refurbish, paint, or stencil on old furniture. Spray paints can cover plastic, laminate, and wood
- Make curtains out of bedsheets or tapestries (check the Web for how-tos)
- Cover boxes and storage trunks with sheets for makeshift tables
- Put up screens or beaded curtains to section off rooms for privacy
- Put washable slipcovers over old chairs, futons, or sofas
- Make your own modern art—splatter paint or blow up photographs and frame them
- Make a collage out of pictures of friends and from magazines. If you have your own loft, glue them right onto the bed.

The Dorm Room Problem/Solution Chart

PROBLEM	SOLUTION
Cold floors	Throw rugs or carpet segments from an outlet store
Your roommate's ugly poster	Sorry, look away
A lack of light	A bendable desk lamp that shines light at different angles; holiday lights
Dry air that's making your skin flake off	A humidifier
Drafts through the windows	Curtains or weather stripping
No space for class projects	Store supplies/projects on a board that slides under the bed
Your bike in the middle of the room	Check into campus bike parking/storage options
Smelliness	Potpourri, room spray, plug-in scents, or actually clean more
A big stain on the carpet	Rearrange your furniture or throw on a carpet square

Do you have that friend who is always looking to steal stuff for his dorm room? He's like an obsessed scavenger. Every time he sees a sign, he's like, "Dude, that would look awesome in my room! Keep an eye out while I go rip it down."

From *Ruminations on College Life* by Aaron Karo, Simon & Schuster, 2002

REAL PEOPLE, REAL DORMS

What's in your room?

Yaffa blocks, car posters, PlayStation 2, and a fridge.
—Mike, University of South Carolina

A flower room with Laura Ashley bed stuff, Monet posters, and stuffed animals.
—Lauren, Capital University (OH)

Glamour room—mostly hot pink, with beads and a big makeup table.
—Alison, University of Massachusetts at Amherst

DORM SCENTS

Sweat, smoke, somebody's tuna sandwich—dorms can *smell*. Some people are more sensitive to smells and can be bothered by them. If that's you, here are some solutions:

- Put a little basket or bowl of potpourri in your room.
- Try an air freshener or baking soda.
- Use a scented plug-in from the candle store (don't use candles themselves; they're a fire risk).
- Get an air purifier, either a small personal one or a room-size one to cleanse the air.
- Open the window, if allowed.

DECORATING TIPS

- Bring in some plants.
- Use decorative bedsheets or blankets as wall hangings.
- Find interesting shower curtains to section off parts of the room.
- Use tension rods for hanging things in doorways and windows without having to use nails or screws.
- Make collages out of the local tabloid's front page, a certain advertising campaign, etc.
- Use holiday lights, now available in all colors—the icicle lights from the ceiling are particularly awesome.
- Create your own art by painting or doing graffiti on large canvases.
- Introduce color by attaching color transparencies, colored lights, and fabric to the walls (try Velcro).
- Use lots of mirrors—You'll always look good, plus they increase the amount of light in a room and give the impression that the room is larger.

—Michael Coleman, director of Student Life at the College for Creative Studies in Detroit, Michigan, and avid HGTV watcher

4

THE DORM'S WATERWAYS

THE BATHROOM

Who'd have thought that the dorm bathroom was important enough to warrant its own section? It does. That's because it's much more than just a place to, uh, *go*. It's a community hub in many dorms—the place you'll meet, greet, and take a seat with your fellow residents.

Some dorms have coed bathrooms, others separate the sexes. At Mount Holyoke (MA), for example, at least one bathroom in each hall is for women only.

At first, some students are concerned about community bathrooms. Community bathrooms, however, are the center of the action on a floor. Students have shared with me that you see everyone in the bathroom—it is the place to catch up on the latest gossip, find out who is involved with what, and discover who likes to take really long showers! You get to see each other getting ready to go out and offer fashion advice. You also get to comfort each other and get into some of the best conversations of your college career as you wait in line. Students who move into areas where there are no longer community bathrooms often miss the tight-knit nature of their community. Overall, it's a great place to get to know others—you see them at their best and at their worst.

—Lisa Brown, assistant director of Residence Life at Xavier University (OH)

BATHROOM SURVIVAL TIPS

Mention dorm bathrooms and the first bit of advice you're bound to hear is: "Wear shower shoes!" Funky, fungal feet aren't the only reason to strap on the flip-flops. You never know if some shards of glass from that broken mirror or a puddle of questionable content might stand in your way. And shower shoes aren't always enough. When multiple people are sharing a space as personal as the bathroom, the following survival tips can go a long way:

- *Don't throw paper towels in the toilet.* They clog it up and can cause a huge mess, complete with bathroom bits flooding the floor.
- *If you see that a sink, shower, or toilet is leaking, let your RA know right away.* Little leaks can often lead to floods, and there's nothing worse than water damage.
- *Dispose of feminine products properly.* Be respectful and hygienic. Enough said.
- *Don't dump your cereal, noodles, or other foodstuffs in the sink.* It'll clog like crazy and stink, too. Plus, you'll get a reputation as "the Noodle Dumper," that person who is way too lazy to toss their food.
- *Beware of water on the floor.* Seemingly "minor" puddles can cause people to wipe out. Clean up the water and you won't have to worry about a floormate hitting his head on the sink.
- *If there's blood in the bathroom, don't touch it.* Contact the staff so, first of all, the bleeding person can be found, and so proper cleanup can occur.
- *Know the alternatives.* Sometimes your floor bathroom may be out of commission, whether for cleaning, repairs, or just because it's full. Find public bathrooms in

your hall for those times when you can't gain access to your own—and can't wait.

- *Get over the fear of the public pee.* There's no getting around it—others will likely be in the bathroom when you have to go. However, just remember that people have enough on their minds, so they probably won't pay any attention to what you're doing, anyhow.
- *Lock your room when you go down to the bathroom.* Don't become an easy target for that thief who can easily learn your patterns and steal your belongings when your room is left unattended.

A fellow Admissions employee at another Midwest institution made a list of things for students to bring with them to school, including "thongs," and kindly shared it with incoming students. After a presentation, though, a student came up to her, upset that she was being told what kind of underwear to wear! The Admissions staffer gently explained that she meant "flip-flops" for the shower where she had listed "thongs," not underwear.

—Troy Moldenhauer, assistant director of Admissions at the University of Wisconsin, Whitewater

BATHROOM BONDING

Yeah, sharing a bathroom with strangers takes some getting used to. But, the positive side is that these folks won't be strangers for long. There's something about holding a conversation with a toothbrush dangling from your mouth that breaks down all possible barriers. Spittle and all, the bathroom is a place for bonding. Take it one step further and hold a "Spa Night" in the bathroom, complete with facial masks, pedicures, and stuff that smells good.

BIG BATHROOM ISSUES

Since it plays such an important part in your daily lives, the bathroom can also be a place where multiple "issues" arise. Discuss your community standards when it comes to bathroom issues *before* they become Big Issues. Agree on how you'll treat this communal space, the cleaning staff, and one another. Take a look at some of the Big Bathroom Issues that you'll need to work through:

- *How will the shower schedule work at peak times?* A lot of people need to get clean before heading off to class, so keep those showers short and sweet.

- *What about paper towels and hand soap?* Many dorm bathrooms don't provide these amenities, simply because they're often used to make a mess rather than cleaning one up. Work with your floor to prove that you *deserve* these items!

- *Who is responsible for cleaning when the drunk person vomits everywhere?* Remember, the cleaning staff isn't there to "clean up after you"; they're there to keep your environment clean and healthy—there's a definite difference!

- *What items are "safe" to leave in the bathroom? And what gets in the way when the cleaning staff is trying to take care of the daily maintenance?* Do all you can to make this person's job easier, not harder. It's a pretty crummy job that many people do with good humor and no complaints. They should be rewarded, not abused!

- *What's the deal when it comes to guests?* Talk with your RA and floormates about how you'll handle opposite-gender guests who need to use a bathroom—can they use yours if someone stands guard or should they go to another floor?

- *How will you handle late-night bathroom noise?* Bathroom door slamming can be problematic for the folks who live close by and who are vibrated awake every time someone visits the restroom at 3 A.M. And bathrooms are notorious echo chambers, too, probably not the best bet for a "private" late-night chat.

—Laurel Christy, community development educator at New York University

WAYS TO GET A BAD BATHROOM REP QUICK!

- Flush all the toilets at once to hear people in the shower squeal.
- Swing open the door and yell things like "Are you done taking a dump *yet*, Gene?"
- Leave gobs of toothpaste in the sink.
- Brush your hair over the sink—and then don't clean your hair out of the drain.
- Put blue Kool-Aid in the shower nozzles so the next person gets a "blue surprise."
- Leave your shaving cream all over the sink.
- Accidentally squeeze lotion on the bathroom floor and then leave it for someone in bare feet to walk on.
- Talk loudly in the bathroom at 3:00 A.M. when you get back from the bar, echoing like crazy for all to hear.
- Leave your scummy hotpot on the shelf for days, with mac-and-cheese residue encrusted on the sides.
- Take extra-long showers, especially if you know there's a line.
- Fail to flush.
- Puke somewhere unflushable.

Bathroom sinks are not meant to be sat on. They will fall off of walls.

>   —Jill Yashinsky, assistant hall director at St. Norbert
>   College (WI)

SUITE BATHROOM ETIQUETTE

Laurel at NYU also encourages students to take the following things into consideration when sharing a smaller bathroom with just a few people:

*   *Toilet-paper politics.* Who buys the TP and how often? What if you have guests who use a lot of toilet paper?
*   *Cleaning supplies.* Who buys them and how often?
*   *Cleaning.* What is the schedule? And what happens if someone doesn't clean at his or her agreed-upon time?
*   *Messes.* What if someone makes an extreme mess and leaves it for someone else, either a suite- or apartment-mate or the regular cleaner, to take care of?
*   *Visitors.* Is it okay for visitors of the opposite gender to use the bathroom?
*   *Personal items.* Can these be left in the bathroom? Are they open for sharing?

COMMUNITY COVER-UPS

Once you get to know your floormates, some modesty tends to fly out the window. That's okay—to a point. It's just that there's a difference between being comfortable and being an exhibitionist. Invest in a robe; it may seem like a hassle to drag it back and forth when you could just go in your towel, but what if there's an Admissions tour going through and you end up being the main attraction? Also consider getting a small, inexpensive fold-up emergency blanket (you can find them in the camping section of Wal-Mart or Target). That way you win if your floor-mates are the kind who think it's hilarious to steal your clothes while you're in the shower!

· ·

THE BASIC BATHROOM BUCKET

The infamous bathroom bucket is where you can store all your shower stuff for easy transport. Get one that's water-proof so you can take it into the shower with you. Make sure it's big enough to hold everything you need:

- Toothbrush/toothpaste
- Shampoo/conditioner
- Soap in a case
- Razor/shaving cream or gel
- Contact lens stuff
- Washcloth or sponge

BATHROOM BUCKET DELUXE

Skeeved out by the bathroom conditions or just looking for extra relaxation and pampering to ease the stress? Add a few items to your bathroom bucket and it'll practically be a spa:

- A loofah
- Scented bath gel or body scrub
- Scented bath lotion
- Face mask
- Back scrubber
- Facial scrub

· ·

This might sound silly, but I underestimated the importance of good pajamas/loungewear before college. Living at home before that, I could wear old nightgowns or frayed pajama pants around family without thinking twice or feeling embarrassed. But once I got to college, I realized that the long trip down the hall to the bathroom in the middle of the night or running out for a fire alarm when someone burned their popcorn necessitated some new, good casual clothing. This sounds so basic to me now, or even superficial, but as a freshman I hadn't thought of this until I got to school, and it really did make a difference in helping me adjust to college life.

—Becky Falto, residence director for Educational Housing
   Services, Inc. (NY)

LAUNDRY LESSONS

When students first come to campus in the fall, everyone usually looks good. They're fit, tan, excited to be here, their clothes are new—campus looks like a walking J. Crew catalog. Then, around October, things begin to get a little gray. Why? It's not because of the weather; rather, it's because most students don't know how to do laundry. To save money, everything goes in one load . . . when it goes in any load at all. Though I don't know the exact physics and chemical interactions involved in this process, what I do know is that when it comes to doing laundry: 1 red shirt + 1 white shirt + hot water = 1 red shirt + 1 pink shirt.

—Jim Carley, associate director for Residential Life at Keene
   State College (NH)

WATER-SAVING

It may feel like there's an endless supply of water, especially in a community setting where hot water tanks hold hundreds of gallons. But water is a valuable resource that needs attention. Get in the water-saving mode now—it's a lifetime habit that will save you money when you're on your own and help save our precious natural resources. Here are some tips:

- Report all drips and leaks right away.
- Consider whether you really need to wash your hair every day.
- Turn off the water while you're brushing your teeth— you only need a little bit at the beginning and at the end of the process.
- Take short showers—this will also ensure that you don't face death stares from others in the shower line, anyhow.
- Don't leave the water running when you're washing dishes—rinse a bunch at a time instead.
- Turn the laundry setting to warm or cold instead of hot.

HOW TO DO LAUNDRY

How did you use to do your laundry? Did you toss it on the floor or in a laundry basket until Mom or Dad came along and took care of it? Face it: You're going to have to do your laundry yourself. And you'd better do it right, or you might end up facing "laundry-mergencies" like white clothes turned colors (!), shredded shorts (!!), or shrunken shirts (!!!). Timi Gleason, an executive coach, gave these tips in my book *Girlwise:*

Step #1—Divide your clothes into piles.

- *Darks.* Colored clothes can bleed dye. If you mix them with white clothes, you may get pink underwear. Darks should be washed in cold water and dried on low temperature, or they could shrink and bleed heavily. Red, dark blue, and purple items are at high risk for bleeding into whites.

- *Whites.* These are fabrics that are completely white, usually cotton, and highly absorbent.

- *Lights.* These are regular-wash fabrics that aren't dark but also aren't white.

- *Delicates.* These can't be washed in a normal cycle. They either need to be hand-washed or put into a delicate cycle in the washing machine, and they usually have to be laid flat to air dry instead of going in the dryer. If washed with regular clothes, the fabric may tear, get a run in it, lose its shape, or shrink. Check the labels; they'll tell you how to wash the garment.

- *Hand-wash items.* Some delicates should *only* be hand-washed, as they are just too delicate to be mixed with heavier items without being ruined. If you aren't sure, be on the safe side. Some hosiery, sweaters, and underwear are too delicate to be put into a machine.

- *Dry-cleaning.* When you are buying your clothes, look at the cleaning requirements before you put your money down. If the label says "Dry Clean," then that's an added expense to think about. These clothes may shrink or lose their shape or bleed their color if washed in water. You can buy kits in the supermarket that effectively dry-clean sweaters and some shirts in your dryer. Jackets and some types of nicer clothing are best taken to a commercial dry cleaner, where they will be pressed and made to look like new again.

Step #2—Load the washing machine.

Set up the washing machine with the right load size and temperature. Start the water running first, and then put in the detergent. (Put in the amount of detergent recommended on the label. Add too much, and your washing machine might overflow with suds. Small loads need less soap. Use your common sense and read the label on the detergent box.) Only when you've added the detergent to the water and let it swish for a second should you put the clothes in. Adding detergent straight on top of clothes causes bleach marks!

Hint: If you notice any rashes on your legs or on your neck, consider that your detergent may be giving you an allergic reaction and that you may be putting too much in (and it's not getting washed out completely).

Another hint: Are your socks disappearing? They could be going out with the washer rinse cycle. If you notice problems, put socks in a mesh bag so they can't escape so easily!

Step #3—Dry.

Put your wet clothes in the dryer. Remember to pull out any clothes that need to be laid flat to dry instead of put in the machine. Toss in any fabric softener sheets you want to use. Always check the lint trap to make sure it's empty. If you don't, the dryer will take forever to dry the clothes.

Wash towels together and don't mix them with sweaters. The sweaters will pick up the lint.

Set up a spot to hang freshly dried shirts and pants so they don't get wrinkled. Remove clothes from the dryer promptly so they can be smoothed out by hand and don't need ironing.

And get yourself a drying rack, too. It saves you dryer funds and

a. prevents that feeling of dryer-crunch your clothes can get

b. preserves your clothes for the long term

c. saves energy

There's something big but often overlooked when it comes to getting used to doing laundry for the first time— remembering to keep an eye on it and pick it up! I've had laundry with my underwear in it left out on the table because I took too long coming to pick it up, and my friends have had things taken when they left their laundry and forgot about it. So protect your property, and don't put people in the position of having to remove your items from a machine. No one wants to have to do that, but no one wants to wait forever to do laundry, either.

—Becky Falto, residence director for Educational Housing Services, Inc. (NY)

HIGH-TECH LAUNDRY

Laundry rooms are going high-tech. Now, in a lot of dorms, you can swipe your ID card to have laundry points deducted instead of hassling with quarters, and you can monitor the availability of washers and dryers via the Internet.

According to the *Chronicle of Higher Education*, several systems—such as e-Suds, Wash Alert System, and LaundryView—are being tested at college sites throughout North America. The technology is fairly simple, as standard washers and dryers emit electronic signals to a laundry-room computer, indicating whether they are in use or experiencing problems. This information is then sent to a server where students can check out machine availability via a Web page.

So, if you have one of these handy systems in place at your school, you'll be able to see how long until the next washer is available before lugging your dirty duds down to the laundry room. Some systems let you put in your e-mail address so you'll receive an e-mail when a machine is ready. Others buzz your cell phone. Sure beats stalking the machines, waiting to grab the next one before somebody else gets to it.

· ·

Freshman: Is excited about the world of possibilities that awaits her, the unlimited vista of educational opportunities, the chance to expand her horizons, and really make a contribution to society.

Senior: Is excited about new dryers in the laundry room.

· ·

TRASH

Like bathrooms and laundry, trash is not something you probably thought too much about before. But if you don't deal with your trash, well, ugh. So check your school's trash and recycling policy. For example, recycling is mandatory at Harvard University (MA), and students are provided specific instructions on how to do it. Students can even see the results of their house's trash bag and recycling standings online. Check with your state/campus recycling regulations since they differ. This is what Harvard tells you to do:

IT'S *EASY* BEING GREEN

At Northland College in Ashland, Wisconsin, students can opt to "go green" in the McLean Environmental Living and Learning Hall. This environmentally friendly building includes photovoltaic (PV) panels on the roof, solar panels, low-emissivity glass windows, and a 120-foot wind generator; it also has linoleum flooring instead of vinyl materials and furniture that is made from recycled plastic. One of the apartments in McLean is even designated as the "Eco House."

Materials should be sorted into trash, mixed paper, commingled container, and battery receptacles.

- Mixed paper includes newspapers, magazines, white and colored office paper (even if it's stapled or taped), flattened cardboard, and even junk mail with window envelopes. It does NOT include food wrappers, tissues, cups, pizza boxes, or trash.
- Commingled containers include cans, jars, cardboard beverage containers, and bottles made of glass, metal, or plastic. All caps and lids should be discarded, and

containers should be emptied and rinsed before they are deposited in the receptacles.

- Batteries of any kind, including those for laptops, cordless phones, pagers, radios, Walkmans, etc., must be recovered for safe disposal.

Find out if your school has a similar policy. If they're still in the dark ages and don't have a recycling policy, lobby to start one.

5

THAT ROOMMATE RELATIONSHIP

Q: What's most new students' #1 concern about dorm life?

A: Who they'll get as a roommate!

Makes sense. After all, you'll be living with this person day in and day out, sharing tight quarters, the DVD player, and your Snapple stash. So, how do you survive this "roommate thing" when you may never have shared a room in your life?

HAVING A ROOMMATE

WHO TO ROOM WITH

Okay, in most cases you really don't get to decide your first year. But you do have *some* say in the matter.

1. The roommate questionnaire

You'll receive a questionnaire at orientation or in the mail. Some of them are really detailed, wanting to know your sleeping and cleaning habits, favorite activities, and what music you like. You might even take a personality test. Others only ask a few basic questions (like if you smoke). Some colleges have an extensive matching system, while others are more random.

Fill it out honestly. No one's going to judge you on whether or not you're a "morning person." Just check the boxes and be yourself.

2. Should you room with a friend?

Your friend from high school is going to college with you. Yeah! That makes it so easy! A built-in roommate . . . or not.

And most experts say *not*. Wait and think before you automatically move in with a friend. Why? Laura Dicke, a Residence Life professional at Vassar College (NY), has this to say about moving in with someone you already know.

- It's harder to feel you can try out new ways of being who you are, and you might feel like you have to keep being your old high school self.

- It's harder to feel you can explore new things at college.

- You might not branch out and meet new people, since you already have a built-in friend to fall back on.

- You might have totally different living habits and end up fighting and possibly losing that person as a friend.

You and your friend already have a relationship that doesn't include *having* to do things, only wanting to do things. It's easier to make up a cleaning schedule with a stranger and make them keep to it!

"Instead of rooming with them, stay connected but also have your own circle," Laura says. Start fresh with a new roommate but request the same hall or one nearby. It's the best of both worlds. You'll develop a social circle and so will your high school bud. You'll still have each other, and you can also be introduced to each other's friends.

If you do leave your roommate pairing up to chance, don't worry. Most schools have good luck matching people who will be compatible, at least when it comes to the major issues. Slogging through the other stuff is part of the excitement and the learning involved when it comes to living with someone new.

HOW THEY PICKED YOUR ROOMMATE

"The push to improve matching roommates took off in the late 1970s when some colleges started using personality tests to identify compatible students," says Gary Schwarzmueller, former executive director of the Association of College and University Housing Officers–International.

Today, most colleges approach the subject one of two ways: "One side says we want roommates similar enough that they get along. Students fill out questionnaires asking about key preferences, typically including smoking, orderliness, study habits, and sleep schedules.

"The other approach to roommate pairing also sorts students according to basic lifestyle preferences, but then puts students together who have some differences. The hope is that they can learn from each other, as well as learn to respect their differences and how to negotiate around them."

—Gary Schwarzmueller quoted in *USA Today,* "Schooled in Compatibility," by Michelle Healy, August 2003

FINDING OUT ABOUT YOUR ROOMMATE

You'll likely get your roommate's name and contact info through the mail. Once you get that roommate letter, it's time to start connecting. You could call, e-mail, or IM the person, or you could even meet up if you live near each other. Some schools are sponsoring online chats for new roommates as well.

Connect in a way that feels comfortable. But don't put it off. Troy Moldenhauer, an assistant director of Admissions and former hall director at the University of Wisconsin, Whitewater, tells why: "I had two first-year students move in together without *ever* talking to each other beforehand," he says. "As a result, they brought two refrigerators, two microwaves, two *big* stereos, two telephones, two computers, two VCRs . . . two of everything. So talk ahead of time—your room just *isn't* that big."

Beyond the stuff issue, connecting with your roommate-to-be can help lay the foundation for a solid relationship once you arrive on campus.

I AM CHARLOTTE SIMMONS

"I'm Beverly. Charlotte?"

Charlotte said hello and managed a smile, but she was already intimidated. This girl was so confident and poised. Somehow she immediately took over the room. *And* she already had friends at Dupont, apparently. They shook hands, and Charlotte said in a timid voice, "These are my folks."

The girl directed her smile toward Daddy, looked him right in the eye, extended her hand, and said, "Hi, Mr. Simmons."

Daddy opened his mouth, but nothing came out. He just nodded deferentially and shook her hand, limply. Charlotte could tell, and she could feel shame weighing down her confidence.

From *I Am Charlotte Simmons* by Tom Wolfe (New York: Farrar, Straus and Giroux, 2004), p. 66

MEETING YOUR ROOMMATE(S)

It can be really awkward meeting your new roommate for the first time. Just meeting someone new in general can be awkward, and now add knowing you're going to live with each other. It's so weird. I mean, you may have shared a room with your brother or sister, but a complete and total stranger? And you're supposed to just walk in the room and be like, hi, this is normal?

First impressions, of course, can be totally wrong. You'll hear stories about who was freaked out by their roommate at first but ended up rooming together for two years. Or the roomies who seemed like twins separated at birth but ended up never speaking again. So instead of driving yourself crazy with questions like Will we like each other? and Will we wind up being in each other's weddings? catch your breath and just connect on a basic level. Like:

- Meet each other's moving crews, whether they're family or friends
- Talk about how to set up the room
- Go get some food
- Roam down your hallway together, meeting other floormates
- Head to the first floor meeting together

Once the floor meeting is done, the unpacking brigade has left, and the dust has settled, you and your roommate will have some time to connect on a deeper level. Time to start discovering who this person is and get a little more info on your living situation.

REAL WORLD

Here are some of the things students told me about move-in day.

"My roommate's mom was making her bed, crying and talking about how she couldn't believe her baby would have to live in these squalid conditions. I was like, um, I'm going to be living here, too, and thanks for pointing that out."

"When he unpacked his music posters I was psyched. We like the same music. We cranked up the stereo. A good start."

"My roommate and I were both really shy. We focused on unpacking and it was really awkward."

"My two roommates were friends from high school. They were talking about their boyfriends, the prom, what they did together this summer. I was totally a third wheel."

"Me and one of the roommates hit it off. I felt a little bad for the other guy, because he could tell he was out of place. He found his own friends later, though."

"I brought a duffel bag with almost everything I owned. My roommate had to bring two cars to fit all his stuff. The difference in our backgrounds was pretty obvious."

Some roommates will be into getting to know you better. They'll want to be friends, or at least find out more about you. They'll be around to hit the dining hall with you. Other roommates will be out of there, meeting people they already know or hitting the library. These types are going to take longer to get to know—if you ever do get to know them at all. Just go with the flow on the roommate situation.

If your roommate seems open and you want to learn a little more about them, try sitting down for some Q&A.

ROOMMATE Q&A

Interests

- What are your hobbies and interests?
- What did you do in high school? Any extracurriculars?
- What kinds of movies do you like? Music? Sports? TV shows?

Background

- Have you ever shared a room with someone before? If so, what was it like?
- Where are you from? What was it like growing up there?
- What do you feel comfortable telling me about your family and friends back home?

College Perspective

- What are you looking forward to here at college?
- What are you nervous about?
- Do you know what your major will be? What do you hope to do with that?

- What types of things are you hoping to get involved with on campus (work-study, soccer team, student government)? How come?

Roommate Issues

- What do you think are the most important things for us to work on as roommates?
- How do you prefer to study—alone or with others? Music on or off?
- Are you more of a morning or a night person? When do you typically go to bed? Wake up?
- How do you feel about having overnight guests?
- What's your take on alcohol, smoking, and other drugs?

From PaperClip Communications' "Roommate Connections" brochure

REALLY QUICK ROOMMATE Q&A

- Major?
- Favorite music?
- Favorite movie?
- Single or attached?
- Siblings?
- #1 TV show to TiVo?
- Any friends on campus?
- Why did you come here?
- Night owl or early bird?

Make a roommate contract that consists of everything from "leaving when the boyfriend is over," to "keeping noise

*down when I am sleeping." It also might help to put both
of your class schedules up, so that you know when each
other is in or out of the room. Having a contract helps you
to follow guidelines, so that you don't end up having fights
over trivial things.*

> —Christin Roberson, community advisor at Alverno College,
>   Milwaukee, WI

GREAT EXPECTATIONS

There's a "best buddy" myth floating around out there
that says all roommates need to be great friends. Yeah, it
sounds good and sometimes winds up being the case. But,
if it doesn't, that's okay, too. Respect and a willingness to
communicate are the keys to surviving and thriving as
roommates. You don't have to hang out with each other;
you just have to be good to each other. It's best to realize
up front that you and your roommate might turn out any
number of ways. Here are some examples of the kind of
roommates you might become.

THE HERE-AND-NOW ROOMMATE. Andy really liked his
roommate, Ben, but they didn't hang out. They both had
other friends at Rowan University (NJ) and other interests. They respected each other, though, and were good
roommates for that moment in time. They haven't talked
since leaving college.

THE NEVER-AGAIN ROOMMATE. Jennifer tried. She really did. But her Clemson (SC) roommate was totally rude
and disrespectful and came with a matching practically live-
in boyfriend. The inevitable blowout came. They didn't
speak for the rest of the semester—or the rest of their lives.

THE RIGHT-AMOUNT-OF-DISTANCE ROOMMATE. Casey's
roommate at the University of Maryland, College Park, was

"very considerate" but had her own life. "We would chat in our room but not get deeply into each other's lives," Casey explains. "I think the fact that we didn't have a lot in common or friends in common actually made us good roommates."

THE EX-FRIENDS ROOMMATES. Melissa and Andrea were part of a group of best friends in high school. They figured rooming together at Ohio State would bring them even closer. Instead, they ended up fighting over cleaning, guys, and studying. Melissa moved out after one semester. They don't talk anymore.

THE "LIFERS." Some people, like Stephie and Sandy, do wind up as longtime friends, even after their roommate days are over. As roommates at Harpur College (now Binghamton University in New York) during the '60s, they spent three years together. Today, after raising their families in separate cities, they still make a point to stay connected and close by taking trips for their "milestone" birthdays, keeping in phone contact, and sending each other frequent "I'm thinking of you" items.

When it comes to roommate relationships, great expectations might let you down. Instead, have *realistic* expectations and a genuine enthusiasm for opening yourself up to someone new. Roommates don't need to have everything in common. Different people can live together and learn from each other's experiences.

We had a match that seemed perfect, until we discovered that one was a cattle rancher's son and the other was a vegan.
—Leslie Marsicano, of Davidson College in North Carolina, on finding roommates for new students, quoted in *Newsweek* (August 18, 2003)

CONNECTING POSITIVELY

Sometimes when you want to fit in, it can be quick and easy to bond over negative things. Will you and your roommate

- gossip about other people as your means of making "small talk"?
- only bond by abusing alcohol or other drugs?
- vandalize stuff together?
- practically have contests to see who can sleep the latest, skip the most classes, and be the best slacker?

Yeah? If so, rethink that bond. Negative bonding is obviously not good for you, and it can backfire. If you and your roommate bond by talking behind your next-door neighbor's back, he might get back at you by blasting music all night. And will it be a fun bonding experience to flunk out or get arrested together?

The good news is that there are plenty of positive ways to connect.

- Share good memories of high school.
- Have an in-dorm scavenger hunt (invite other rooms and team up with your roommate).
- Start an intramural team.
- Share career goals and support each other.
- Have a study night in the study room.
- Get off campus and go to a local festival.
- Work on a service project together.
- Start an informal volleyball night.
- Do "sneak attack" nice things for people on your floor.

So you want to throw a party in your room with your roommates? A small get-together is probably okay, but an all-out party gets tricky in some instances. Check with your RA or look at your dorm policy on what's allowed at parties—and what's not. For one thing, you can't just host a zillion people in your room. Two words: fire code. So your RA might suggest you throw a party in your lounge instead. Work with your RA to make it a community thing rather than something that disrupts people.

Once you've got the party okayed, try these suggestions:

- Set a budget. It might not take much, but factor in paper cups, munchies, etc.

- Pick a date. You might want to schedule when there's an away game or during the first weekend back after break.

- Pick a theme—Super Bowl, '80s, costume, murder mystery, dressy . . .

- Make the invitation list. Try to include as many people from your floor as you can so nobody feels left out. You can always stagger the times if you think it's going to be too crowded.

- Pick the music, pick your outfit, and get the food. You're ready.

Pre-party: Your roommate(s) and maybe a couple close friends will come over early to set up, which in a dorm usually doesn't require much. So it's usually just hanging out and starting early.

Party: Everyone who shows up when they're supposed to.

After-party: After most people have gone home, there will still be the core group of partyers, plus stragglers and people who show up really late. They'll hang in your room, probably until you kick them out.

Share your home with each other. If possible, bring each other home for a holiday or weekend. Learn about the home environment. It may help everyone have a clearer perspective of families, friends, and their strengths and weaknesses.

—Gretchen Dobson, Alumni Relations officer at Tufts
   University (MA)

CO-DORM-PENDENCE

Sometimes students can depend on their roommates *too* much. Gretchen Yeninas, the director of Residence Life at Wilkes University in Wilkes-Barre, Pennsylvania, recounts how she had a student come in with wild expectations for what her roommate relationship would be like. "She bought a cell phone for her roommate so they could be on the same plan. She had never had a sister or brother so she was excited to have one." However, the roommate did not reciprocate these almost smothering, albeit good-intentioned, feelings. The expectant roommate floundered with disappointment. We can't force roommates to want the same things we want. Living together is a learned skill that grows with time.

COMMUNICATE WITH YOUR ROOMMATE

The Holy Grail of roommate relations is communication. Just ask any college administrator who has seen numerous roommates flop or flourish. It pretty much boils down to this: When students commit to communicate, they can make it. When they start complaining behind each other's backs and stop talking, things can get ugly. Fast.

SET SOME GROUND RULES

Right after you move in, before any of this becomes a problem, talk about things and set some rules you both want to follow:

Sleep Patterns

- When do you like to go to bed? When do you wake up?
- If your roommate is trying to sleep, what is the acceptable level of noise or light?

Leaving Each Other Messages
(Phone, People Stopping By, Roommate-to-Roommate)

- Will you have a regular place to post messages?
- Will you let each other know where you are when you're gone for longer periods of time?

Studying in the Room

- Can you study with other people around or do you need quiet?
- Is it okay to have the TV or music on?

Having Guests

- If one roommate is studying, what should happen?
- Can guests use your roommate's bed/chair/desk when they aren't there?
- Overnight guests—yes or no? Same-sex only?

Setting Up the Room So You Both Feel Comfortable

- Anything in the room that's offensive to the other (mooing alarm clocks, posters with naked people)?
- How do you both feel about what equals "messy" and what is/isn't acceptable cleanlinesswise?

- What will you do with food, laundry, bedding, trash, etc., in the room to avoid odor, bugs, and grossness?

Other Policies

- Is it okay to have alcohol or other drugs in the room?
- Is either roommate doing anything the other thinks is unsafe?

Dining Hall

- Do you want to eat together at some meals?
- Should you wait for your roommate for meals?

Using Shared Items

- Is anything off-limits?
- If you're sharing a computer, who gets "first dibs" —the owner or whoever has something due first?
- If something breaks, how will you handle it?
- Can you borrow each other's clothes, sports equipment, CDs, etc.? Do you need to ask first?

Handling the Phone

- When is it too late to make or receive a phone call?
- If your roommate is studying, will you take a call elsewhere?
- Will you keep your long-distance bills separate by each having personal identification numbers?
- How will voice mail and messages be handled?

Managing the Alarm Clock

- Do you expect your roommate to wake you up if you sleep through your alarm?

- What are your snooze-button habits? What's acceptable to the other person?
- Will you both use the same clock or have your own?

· ·

YOUR CALL

Here's what former students told me:

- "My new roommate pulled out a two-page roommate contract he'd written himself. I was expected to agree with him on things like how far the blinds should be pulled down at certain hours of the day. Uh . . . I don't think so."
- "My new roommates and I ordered pizza and went through a list of questions we got at orientation. We asked each other funny questions, too, so it was fun. And took care of a lot of issues that might have come up later in a laid-back way."
- "My roommate told me she needed all the lights on when she studied—even all night. She was so intimidating I was like, okay, and bought a sleep mask."
- "My roommate wanted his girlfriend to sleep over— every single night. I had to say no, but I didn't want to piss him off. So I joked that she was so hot I might not be able to control myself. He laughed and we agreed on weekends only."

· ·

As you can see, there's a lot to talk about! Be up front and get these things out in the open early on so you can be proactive in avoiding potential conflicts. You'll be glad you did!

Communication with your roommate does not happen through telepathy.

> —Zachariah R. Newswanger, area coordinator for
> Terraces/Towers at Ithaca College (NY)

AVOID MULTIPLE MAYHEM

Getting to know one or two roommates seems like a challenge, but some students have even more. At the College for Creative Studies in Detroit, Michigan, students typically live in suites of three to eight people each. Michael Coleman, director of Student Life at the school, says that if you're living with more than one person, there are more issues you should discuss on top of the usual ones:

- Can certain foods, like ketchup, milk, and more, be shared? Who should buy these things?

- What happens if you are the last person out of the suite but you're not sure if your roommates have their keys?

- What type of cleaning schedule will you set up, especially when it comes to shared spaces like the bathroom, kitchen, and living room?

- Where does mail for everyone in the suite go?

- Whose name should go on accounts and how do you make sure that person doesn't get stiffed when it comes to bill-paying time?

- What areas of the suite are designated as shared areas? Which ones are private sleeping areas?

- Who should do dishes? How long after dishes are used should they be washed?

Getting along with multiple roommates can be much trickier than getting along with just one. More personalities and more schedules make everything a little more complicated . . . and possibly a little more fun, too.

REAL WORLD:
WHAT STUDENTS TOLD ME

"I lived in a suite with two other girls. I felt really left out. They went out together and never invited me, and they all talked about it in front of me. It was like I didn't exist. I had to deal with it all year."
  —Michelle

"I lived with three other roommates. I became really good friends with two of them. The other one was seriously annoying, but she glommed on to us. She wanted to room with us the next year, too. We had to be honest with her—we wanted a triple without her, but we tried to be sensitive about it at least."
  —Trina

"We all pretty much hated each other. I just had to figure out everyone's schedule and then avoid them as much as possible."
  —Caroline

"At first I wasn't happy, there were four of us in a room that was made to be a double, but we ended up getting along. We moved into a suite and stayed roommates all four years."
  —DeVonn

I had four suitemates. One was a snorer. One, a sleepwalker and talker. The other one, a sleep around with everyone. It was an interesting year.
—El, Boston University (MA)

VISITORS

One of the biggest differences of not living at home is that you can have anyone over. Before, you had to live by your parents' rules of who could visit and stay over. Now it's up to you. Which means it's easy to abuse your freedom. Will you encounter (or be) any of these people:

- The roommate who's so excited to have her boyfriend sleep over that he practically moves in.
- The guy who busts in without knocking.
- The girl who can't stand her roommates so she lives in your room.
- The guy who brings the party back to your room after the bars close.
- The friend from home who doesn't go to college but who comes to stay—every weekend.

Visitors can be a touchy subject. Now that you don't need your parents' permission to have people over any-time and just because you *can* have a sleepover every night, doesn't mean you should. Take into consideration the dorm's rules (some don't allow overnight guests of the opposite sex, some don't allow overnight guests at all) and your roommate's preferences, as well as your own val-ues and whether you're getting enough sleep and being productive. If you do have visitors, remember that guests who stay any longer than a couple of days will get old REAL fast.

The biggest issue in the visitors department? Getting

"sexiled." One roommate wants to hook up, and the other roommate is stuck looking for another place to hang—or sleep for the night. It doesn't happen to everyone, but when it does, it can be a challenge.

REAL WORLD: SEXILED

sex•iled   Banished from the room because your roommate is engaging in intimate relations with someone else.

- We did the sock thing. If one of us didn't want to be disturbed, we'd tie a sock on the door. Of course, it sucks to come back from class wanting to crash or something and see the sock. But it ended up pretty equal.
- I hated being asked to leave my own room. But I didn't think I could do anything about it, so I just slept in the lounge. The RA finally saw me camping out there and had a talk with my roomie.
- I just wasn't comfortable with it. My roommate wasn't happy about that and put himself on a list for a single.
- It was a pain. But I just dealt with it.
- We made a schedule that worked around both our classes. I didn't necessarily use it to be with someone; sometimes I used my time for alone time.

DEALING WITH DIFFERENCE

Obviously your roommate is not going to be your identical twin. You'll have different backgrounds, likes, dislikes, and all that. And while you may be from a little town while your roommate grew up in the city, it doesn't mean you can't figure a way to get along. After all, Superman and Mrs. Doubtfire found a way to cohabitate during their days at Juilliard and remained friends. That's right, actors Christopher Reeve and Robin Williams were roommates back in the day. And that combination, surprisingly, worked.

To bridge the gap, talk with your roommate about what it means to be a vegan, a Jewish guy, an Asian athlete, a bisexual, an honors student—whatever it is that helps define you. Recognize that we all have multiple labels and differences that make up the whole of who we are. You're not easy to define and neither is your roommate. And that's okay—it's what getting in touch with differences is all about. Your world is bound to open as a result of your roommate relationship, so think of it that way.

Kelly Schaefer, a former hall director and current assistant director of the DePaul University (IL) Student Center, says it comes down to being up front and letting your roommate know what you're about. If you're uncomfortable having alcohol in the room because you're underage and a policy violation could screw up your record, then stand up for yourself. "Identify those specific behaviors you find hard to handle," she suggests. Focus on those and plan to let little issues slide.

You may find yourself rooming with someone whose language, culture, and approach to life are *way* different from yours. Those things that may seem so drastically different at the start can wind up being the cause of some of your most positive growth experiences in college. See "The Difference Made by Difference" on page 135 for more about how to get the most out of a friendship with a student from another culture or background.

YOU AS A ROOMMATE

One thing students tend not to remember is who they are as a roommate. They often lose perspective because they're so wrapped in their own issues.

—Kelly Schaefer, former hall director and current assistant director of the DePaul University (IL) Student Center

Complaining about your roommate's late hours? Maybe he's hating your snooze-button obsession. Roommate's sloppiness making you crazy? Maybe your habit of borrowing her clothes is right back at ya. Before you go bitching to everyone you know about your roommate, remember, the problems may not be entirely one-sided. Once you get in the dorm and get settled, take this quiz to find out how you stack up as a roommate.

The last time I was pissed with my roommate, I

a. didn't say anything but erased her messages and pretended voice mail ate them.

b. yelled at her and said things that shouldn't be printed here.

c. talked it out, even though I was a little uncomfortable starting the conversation.

When it comes to room cleanup, my philosophy is

a. spotless—and I'll be giving my roommate lessons on how to clean just right.

b. it's college! We're supposed to be disgusting.

c. I'm pretty neat, but I'm willing to let my roommate's bad days slide.

Roommate's crush stops by. Crush turns out to be hot. I

   a. invite the crush in to wait even though my
   roommate is out of town for a week.

   b. tell her the roommate is out with his new
   girlfriend, but that I'll buy her a drink.

   c. tell her I'll let my roommate know she stopped
   by—and that's all.

Yeah! My high school sweetie is coming to visit. I'll

   a. tell my roomie she needs to leave for the
   weekend.

   b. tell her? It's my room, too. Sweetie can just
   show up.

   c. book a hotel room and invite my roomie to stop
   over for dinner with us.

Roommate broke up with his girlfriend.

   a. Oh well. She was in our room too much, anyway.

   b. I'll tell him to get over it; he's depressing me.

   c. I'll bring munchies and stay home and cheer
   him up.

*My roommate makes weird embarrassing noises when
sleeping. I*

   a. do a great imitation for my friends. Hey,
   it's funny.

   b. invite everyone from the floor for a midnight
   showing.

   c. think about what I might be doing in *my* sleep
   and don't say a word.

If you answered mostly

- **a:** You're a little high-strung and, shall we say, passive-aggressive?
- **b:** There's no passive—all aggressive. Time to rethink those roommate skills or be prepared to pay for a single next year.
- **c:** Maybe this was a little obvious, but yes, you're a good roommate.

She was from my high school but we weren't friends then. I was the cheerleader/snob, and she was the band girl/valedictorian. I agreed to room with her because I thought she'd just sit there and study and not bug me. We wound up becoming the best of friends, and stereotypes and cliques of high school became irrelevant. We are inseparable today.

—Julia, student at Miami University (OH)

BEING A CONSIDERATE ROOMMATE

There are so many ways to be considerate; it just takes some thinking about your roommate's needs as well as your own:

SHARE WITHOUT TAKING ADVANTAGE. Know what's off-limits. And even if it's within limits, borrow a little of something but not a lot. Borrow a squirt or two of toothpaste if you run out, or borrow a bowl of cereal, but don't eat the entire box.

PERFORM THE BEHAVIOR FAVOR. If your roommate needs a ride to the bus station, help her find one. If she asks for a piece of information, try to get back to her as quickly as you can. When you share the Behavior Favor with your roommate, chances are that she'll reciprocate in kind. This creates a healthy synergy of give-and-take between the two of you.

PUT YOURSELF IN THEIR SHOES (BIRKS, HEELS, NIKES . . .). None of us can know what someone else goes through on a day-to-day basis. But try to increase your awareness of what your roommate's life is like. What's his family scene? Is he struggling with any classes? Does he get wicked headaches? By asking a few simple questions and keeping your eyes open, you can better understand what he's about.

BE HONEST AND UP FRONT. If something's bugging you, let your roommate know rather than talking behind her back. Don't make up excuses or avoid her. Honesty between roommates can be the difference between someone trusting you and someone wondering if you have a hidden agenda.

Consideration is the key. Just *asking* can make a difference, and if your roommate is even close to a decent person, they'll try to accommodate you. When you answer the phone, *ask* if your long conversation will disrupt your roommate's studying. Before you borrow her CD, *ask* if it's okay. Before going out to grab food, *ask* if you can pick anything up for him. It's polite and your roommate will want to be considerate to you, too.

But don't give in TOO much. If you compromise so much that you're always giving in to someone else's wishes at the cost of your own, then you've gone too far and you're just a doormat. Bend back a bit the other way, assert yourself, and stand up for your rights. Keep ownership over things that are important to you while remaining a considerate roommate.

WAYS TO ANNOY YOUR ROOMMATE

Tried to solve your problems and work through your differences and you're still hating the roomie? Here are some ways to have a little fun with a bad situation.

- Every time your roommate walks in, yell, "Hooray! You're back!" as loud as you can and dance around the room for five minutes. Afterward, keep looking at your watch and saying, "Shouldn't you be going somewhere?"

- Get some hair. Disperse it around your roommate's head while he is asleep. Keep a pair of scissors by your bed. Snicker at your roommate every morning.

- Scatter stuffed animals around the room. Put party hats on them. Play loud music. When your roommate walks in, turn off the music, take off the party hats, put away the stuffed animals, and say, "Well, it was fun while it lasted."

- Make a sandwich. Don't eat it, leave it on the floor. Ignore the sandwich. Wait until your roommate gets rid of it, and then say, "Hey, where's my sandwich?!" Complain loudly that you are hungry.

- Late at night, start conversations that begin with, "Remember the good old days, when we used to . . ." and make up stories involving you and your roommate.

From a list going around on the Internet

Find out early what makes your roommate tick. The following conversation starters can help you both figure out each other's pet peeves:

- Don't take it personally, but I'm touchy about . . .
- I get stressed out when . . .
- When people gossip or make derogatory comments about someone else, I tend to . . .
- Some of the causes I feel passionately about include . . .
- A few things that really annoy me are . . .
- When I'm angry, I show it by . . .

Talk now rather than finding things out the hard way.

NO MESS!

What's one of the biggest complaints of roommates everywhere? Messy roommates. Stanford University (CA) helps ward off this issue by offering cleaning services. Students can have their dorm room cleaned for $20 weekly, every other week, monthly, or one time only. Okay, that sounds really, really good.

I had always had my own room growing up and didn't realize how some of the things I did would really make my roommates mad. Like if I had an 8:00 A.M. class and I was getting ready and my roommate was still sleeping, I thought nothing of it to turn the lights on and get ready and blow-dry my hair right there in our little dorm room. To me, I can sleep through anything, and if she did the same it would never bother me one bit, but it drove her crazy. She never said anything for like six months and then she blew up. I was shocked and had no idea. I now realize that I was an idiot and should have gone down to the bathroom like everyone else did to get ready when their roomies were sleeping.

—Teressa, Penn State (PA)

My roommate Serena and I were such different people. She was completely nocturnal. When the year first began, she would start studying when I hopped into bed for the night. She didn't want to go to the commons to study, but I couldn't stand the bright overhead light being on while I was trying to fall asleep. So we compromised. Serena bought a much dimmer desk lamp. She could study, I could sleep. But it was all about compromising between the two of us. That's what made it work. It also helped that we went out together on the weekends!

—Allison, Public Information officer at Penn State (PA)

ROOMMATES FROM HELL

Roommate horror stories. The nude sleeper, the copycat, the missing-her-boyfriend-from-home weeper, the obsessive fraternity pledge chanting at 2:00 A.M., the computer addict whose computer glows all night long. They're not so funny while you're living with them. But, okay, they make good stories after you survive them. Check out these worst-case scenarios told to me by former students:

- I lived in a triple. My two roommates fought all the time. They put masking tape in the middle of the room. Since I was a neutral party, I got to go into either section, but they weren't allowed to set foot on the other's side.

- First it was my watch missing. Then some of my CDs. And my clothes. Then I realized how my roommate was funding his online gambling habit.

- He did booty call every night. With different girls. Then they'd call all the time or wait outside our room, all freaked out when he didn't call them back.

- My roommate. Her boyfriend. Noise. Enough said.

- She snuck her cat in and begged me to let it stay. It would howl and scratch at everything. I spent so much time trying to hide the cat from the floor staff.

- He didn't shower. Ever.

- He used my toothpaste, my towels, my deodorant, and, yes, I caught him with my toothbrush.

- She would conveniently be there when my boyfriend stopped by between classes. Wearing little teeny tank tops and shorts. He is no longer my boyfriend—he's hers.

Take time for yourself! Living with roommates can be very difficult at times, but having a place that you can go and get away from it for a while is important. Find a corner in the library, a bench around campus, or someplace to relax and take some time for you!

—Jenna Zemrak, resident assistant at Keene State
College (NH)

SAFE SPACE

Depending on your background, safety may mean one thing to you and another thing to your roommate. The bottom line, though, is that you're both responsible for the safety of the people and things inside your shared space. So, talk about safety concerns, such as:

- Allowing people to enter your room when no one is there
- Locking the door
- Using illegal and/or unsafe items (like halogen lamps, candles, incense)
- Sharing passwords and phone PINs
- Carrying keys with your ID on a key chain (dangerous if someone finds the keys and knows what door they open!)
- Hosting overnight guests

The decisions you make about these and other safety issues impact your roommate, too.

WHEN YOUR ROOMMATE IS STRUGGLING

Perhaps your roommate hasn't been sleeping well or is having a tough time with calculus. Maybe he's been exhibiting an angry streak lately or maybe she has been crying a lot.

Should you try to help or be hands-off? Sitting back and watching your roommate suffer is obviously pretty harsh. If the problem is minor or temporary, think of ways to help your roommate get through it. Ask what you can do to help them through the situation. And listen. Most often a kind ear goes a long way to helping them feel less alone.

Here are some suggestions for cheering up your roommate after a minor downer.

- Take him out for pizza or a movie
- Encourage her to leave the room if she's holed up
- Drag him out to a good party
- Invite over some friends she likes

Some of us experience a tinge of hero complex, wanting to jump to the rescue when we see someone struggling. No matter how noble your intention to help, though, you have to recognize your limitations in the helping role. Some things are better handled by a trained professional.

Does your roommate need professional help? Here is some advice to help you figure out if what's bothering your roommate is really serious.

- Be aware of what "normal" behavior is for your roommate. When someone is having trouble coping for any reason, they often act outside of their normal pattern. Be on the lookout for changes in sleeping or eating behaviors, excessive crying or anger, or sometimes a lack of emotion entirely.
- Talk confidentially with your residence hall staff to ask for advice and connections to campus resources.
- Guard her privacy. If your roommate is experiencing issues that the rest of your community is aware of, then you might be asked questions like "What's happening with your roommate?" Don't blab, you'll lose her trust.
- Seek support from someone you can talk with, but unless you're talking to someone who is bound by confidentiality, the focus should be on sharing your feelings. Don't share secrets.
- Be honest about what your needs are. For example, if your roommate is disrupting your own sleep or study habits, it's completely okay to say, "I want to help you as much as I can, but at some point I have to rest. When you're awake during the night, can we agree on what the noise level can be in the room?"
- Be aware of your own limits. At what point are your roommate's issues simply too large for you to live with

daily? If your own stress level and academics are being affected, share this with your hall staff and ask for assistance.

—Kathy Hobgood, an assistant director of Housing for Residence Life at the University of Florida

HANDLING CONFLICT

Conflict is inevitable. That point gets repeated a lot, but I think people need to really cozy up to that concept before they can work to resolve it. Be ready for conflict to happen. No matter how much you love your roommate, you are going to disagree on things. It's normal, natural, and you should look forward to it in some perverse way because, if handled properly, conflict is a "creative opportunity," a chance to reexamine a problem and come up with a novel solution.

> —John Delconte, organizational development/dialogue consultant and volunteer at the Dispute Settlement Center of Orange County (NC)

So, you and your roommate have hit a snag, eh? Conflict has reared its head and things aren't going so smoothly. Yup, it happens.

That's right, conflict doesn't have to spell out disaster. It's a natural part of the process, especially when people are living in close quarters as roommates. How you choose to handle the conflict is the key! Temper tantrums, bottled-up feelings, or the silent treatment may be your instincts, but the reality is that conversation and compromise typically do the trick *much* more effectively.

. . . .

DON'T TRY THIS AT HOME

If your roommate is struggling, there are a few things you can do that will likely make a situation worse:

- Don't secretly call your roommate's family in an attempt to "fix" things—you never know if family issues are the *cause* of her problems. Check with your college counseling resources first.
- Don't give too much advice—if your roommate follows what you say and the results are disastrous, he'll point the finger of blame at you.
- Don't get into a serious conversation when either you or your roommate are drunk or high—the level of rationality goes out the window when people are in an altered state.
- Don't promise your roommate that you won't tell anyone about her problems—if she's suffering from something more serious than you can handle, the *best* thing you can do for her is to get expert help.

. . . .

Ways to manage conflict:

1. Expect conflicts to happen and don't be overwhelmed by them. Hundreds of people from different backgrounds live together under one roof. Of course conflicts are going to occur. Conflict can be negative or positive, depending on how you look at it. You can see it as an opportunity to get more of what you want, to improve a relationship, or just to bring a little bit of

peace to the earth. If you expect it, then it's not as much of a problem.

2. Recognize perspectives are not right or wrong, but they definitely can be different. That stack of pizza boxes in the corner may seem messy to you, but for your roommate, the fact that they are *stacked* signifies cleanliness and order. Before you go on the attack, put yourself in the other person's shoes (although their shoes might be the problem!). Think about it from their point of view.

3. Chill out. Before you confront someone about a conflict, make sure you're calm enough to have an intelligent conversation. If you're steaming mad, you're less able to think clearly. If you lose your temper, you risk looking foolish or making the situation worse. Take some time and space to calm down. Breathe deeply, count to ten, take a shower, go for a walk. Write down how you feel in a journal. Avoid drugs or alcohol (they may help you relax, but they will not help your ability to think clearly and communicate). If someone confronts you with a lot of anger, acknowledge their feelings ("I can tell you're really upset") and ask if you can talk later. If later isn't possible, ask them to sit down. Offer them something to drink. Do what you can to create a calm situation. If you feel physically threatened or in danger, however, get out of the situation quickly or call for help.

4. Figure out what you want, then consider your options. Your suitemate insists on singing loudly in the shower and it's bothering you that she isn't taking other people's needs into consideration. You have several courses of action. (1) Ignore it, (2) throw a bucket of cold water on her, (3) try to communicate with her about it, and

(4) sing along! Okay, maybe not. You'll have to consider what's realistic, what you're willing to do, and what could actually help the situation. If you want her to consider other people's needs, making her mad probably won't help. If you try to talk it out with the other person, keep the next few steps in mind.

5. Make time and space for conversation. If you're going to talk it out, avoid starting the conversation five minutes before you have to go to class. Figure out a time and place that will be good for you and the other person. You may want to meet on neutral ground, like at the dining hall. Before you start talking about the problem, it might be helpful to set up some ground rules that you both agree to follow. A few to think about are: no interrupting, no name-calling or put-downs, and agreeing to work on the problem. This may seem kind of hokey, but it can really help. Just say, "Before we start, I just want us to both agree not to interrupt each other. Is that okay?"

6. Tell your side (all of it), then listen to the other person. Telling your roommate that he needs to "get off the @#*!ing phone!" may let him know that you are upset, but it doesn't explain *why*. Communication is less helpful when we only tell part of the story. Try to include these four pieces of information when telling your side:

   • What's bothering you. "When you're on the phone this late . . ."

   • Any emotions that you are feeling. "I feel upset, bothered, annoyed . . ."

   • Why it bothers you and what effect it has on your life. "Because I can't sleep and I have a test tomorrow."

   • What you'd like to change. "Can you find

another time or place to talk?" By giving the other person more information, they are more likely to understand what you want. They might not give it to you, but at least you've done your best to communicate. It may be helpful to write some of your thoughts down ahead of time so that when you get to the conversation, you are clear about what you want to say.

7. Brainstorm solutions. Come up with as many ideas to resolve the conflict as you can before deciding which ones are good or bad. Write them down on a piece of paper. If you shoot down an idea right away, the person who came up with it will probably be less enthusiastic about trying to work with you. If you don't like their idea, suggest an alternative. "So your idea is that I wake up at six A.M. every morning to clean the room? Okay, that's one idea. Here's another—I could clean the room in the afternoon after classes. Any other ideas?"

8. Go for a win-win and then check in. Look for ways that both people can benefit from a resolution. This takes more time and effort, but the resolution is more likely to stick if both people feel like they got something out of it. After you come up with a solution, set up a time to check in with the other person to make sure that things are working out for both of you. If there are problems, stay calm and keep talking, listening, and brainstorming.

9. Recognize that electronic communication is tricky. E-mail or instant messaging may seem like an easy way to express yourself in a conflict. However, it is very easy to misinterpret what someone says when it is just words on a screen. It can also be insulting to e-mail someone who lives in the same room as you, so it could make

things worse. When the other person is not standing in front of you, it may be tempting to really let them have a piece of your mind. You could use electronic communication to invite a face-to-face conversation. Be courteous and brief, and avoid words in all caps or profanity.

10. Watch out for the conflict "triangle." You have a problem with your roommate and want to talk to a friend about it. That's okay. Ask yourself: Will they spread this to other people and make the situation worse? Will this person listen to me? What do I want from this person—advice, a shoulder to cry on, someone to help me talk to my roommate? Also consider the other person. You are asking for their help, so be considerate and appreciative.

11. Ask for help. Residence Life staff or campus counselors often receive training in helping people resolve conflicts. Most will offer mediation services where you can have an objective person help you try to work through your issues together. Some campuses even have mediation centers. A mediator will not take sides or tell you what to do. He will help you communicate with your roommate and figure out your own solution.

12. Recognize that the only person you can change is yourself. As much as you'd like to fix your roommate's annoying habits, the only person you can control is YOU. Improve your communication skills. Do your best to stand up for your needs while being kind and respectful. You may not get along with everyone, but you might be surprised at how your behavior can inspire others to change themselves.

—Joe Hensley, youth coordinator with the Dispute Settlement Center of Orange County (NC)

TALK—IN PERSON

In order to survive a roommate conflict, you've got to face it. And I mean face it in *person*. "Don't leave notes about things like dirty dishes, laundry pileups, etc.," Michael Coleman, director of Student Life at the College for Creative Studies (MI), cautions. "The tone you write a note in and the tone that someone reads it in can be *completely* different." Misunderstandings often arise when roommates resort to note writing, he says.

Don't hide behind technology. It's best not to handle things by leaving a passive-aggressive away-message on your instant messenger saying, "I'm out of the room because it's *always* too loud in here!" Holly Alexander Agati, assistant director for Programming at the College of William & Mary (VA), stresses, "Don't just sit in the same room and IM each other, pounding on the keyboard." Holly has seen roommates put up this technological wall, making true conflict resolution impossible because the players aren't willing to confront each other. "So much of it is about having an open dialogue with your roommate," she says. It's important to come out from behind that virtual curtain and deal with things head-on.

What if the other person refuses to talk about the problem? "The 'silent treatment' is a favorite coping strategy for many people in conflict," says Joe Hensley, youth coordinator with the Dispute Settlement Center of Orange County (NC). He suggests the following to kick-start the conversation:

- Start on a different topic, something easy; then, once you're talking, you may eventually be able to shift the subject to the problem at hand.

- Make sure that you're doing a good job of listening when someone does talk. Let them know that you want to hear what they have to say.
- Ask open-ended questions that can't be answered with just a yes or a no.

PEOPLE CAN CHANGE

So your roommate is driving you crazy with his pranks? The girl down the hall is so stuck-up she never once said hi? The shy kid who never leaves his room . . . what's his name?

Don't rule them out forever. You've heard it before: college is a time of growth, of maturing, and blah blah. But it's really true. That roommate might end up calming down and could be the best lab partner ever your senior year. That girl might realize her snotty ways aren't working like they did in high school and end up as your friend and favorite apartmentmate. The shy kid could get more comfortable and end up as your hall president the next year.

You never know.

SHOULD I STAY OR SHOULD I GO?

When things get rough, the flight reflex often kicks in. "I've had enough, I want out," you may be thinking. But in these days of packed dorms, moving may not always be an option. So, what now? You could do what my twin sister did and dump a trash can of garbage on her nasty roommate's top bunk, but er, no. That won't help. But these things might.

- Talk with your RA for ideas on how to handle your situation.
- Put things in perspective. Sometimes a problem that seems *huge* this week turns into barely a blip the next.

- Remind yourself that it's not forever.
- Try having a roommate mediation with your RA or residence hall staff mediating.
- See if someone else having a roommate conflict wants to swap roommates.
- Put yourself on a waiting list and, in the meantime, work on keeping things civil and respectful with your current roommate.

One thing that is typically advised against is getting your parents involved. You're in college now, and the expectation is that you'll work to resolve your own issues and take responsibility for your life. Just know that *you* can go to your RA and your hall director and ask for assistance. They're not going to listen to your parents more than they'll listen to you. Not that you can't bounce around ideas with your parents, but it's time to handle things yourself.

One thing that typically is a deal-breaker for roommates is when values just don't match—if you find your roommate cheating, lying, doing drugs, hooking up every night, or doing anything you completely disagree with on a moral level, it might be best to simply put in your names for a switch and lay low until it happens.

Dan Phillips recalls when his roommate at SUNY Oswego stole cans of food from the dorm's holiday can-drive box. "I saw another friend of mine putting those cans in the box that morning," he recalls, "and when I got back to my room, three of the four cans were sitting on top of the fridge. My roommate had taken them and eaten one already." He snuck the other three cans back to the box, and when his roommate asked about it, Dan confronted him. An argument and a physical fight ensued. In this kind of situation, moving out might be the best option.

And if you're feeling unsafe in your room for any reason (your roommate drunk-kickboxes, deals drugs, stalks you, etc.), get the hall staff involved right away. You should *never* have to feel threatened in your own space. So, go to the people who live right in the dorm with you and who have been professionally trained to handle these types of situations.

THE ROOMMATE DIVORCE

Switching roommates. You've made the decision. (Or your roommate made the decision.) It can be like a divorce. Sometimes it's totally amicable, and you guys go off on your own and say a friendly hi when you see each other on campus. Other times it's harder—complete with screaming matches and custody battles (like who gets the futon you both bought).

The good news is, no matter how much your roommate situation sucks, nobody is forced to have the same roommate for more than a year. And most colleges even allow room transfers midyear when there's space. Different residence halls have different policies. Some residence halls have a "freeze" period where students must stick it out for a certain length of time before they can petition for a room change. If it's a mutual room exchange, like you and another person want to trade roommates and all parties agree to switch rooms, probably any dorm will let you do it. If you or your roommate want to leave and don't have a swap ready, you'll have to submit a housing-request change. You'll likely have to explain why you want to make the move. If housing officials agree that your reasons are valid, you may be reassigned or placed on a waiting list. There may be a fee involved, though, so make sure this is your only option.

START A ROOMMATE TRADITION

1. Keep your holiday tree up year-round and decorate it for all the different seasons—there just aren't enough Groundhog Day trees these days!

2. Be known for having the best daily quotes on your wipe-off memo board.

3. Do room themes like Heavy Metal Month or Penguin Power and decorate accordingly.

4. Host bizarre film fests every month with a different theme (this month, Cheesy Movies Featuring Actors Named Ron; next month, Movies Where Animals Do Bad Things).

5. Have a designated "Destressor Zone" in your room, whether it's a beat-up old chair or a kiddie pool you inflate for just this purpose.

6. Road-trip a few times each semester to visit out-of-the-ordinary places in the community.

7. Volunteer at the Humane Society together as dog walkers.

8. Create a room voice mail message, say, one that mixes Jessica Simpson and the Simpsons, and change it every week.

9. Challenge yourselves to get a great grade in a tough class and celebrate after you both do.

10. Set up study times together finishing off with a pizza delivery.

THE ROOMMATE'S BILL OF RIGHTS AND RESPONSIBILITIES

All roommates have the right:

1. To privacy
2. To respect
3. To open communication
4. To mutually clean living quarters
5. To personal safety and security of possessions
6. To have comfortable sleep and study conditions
7. To be asked before their possessions are used
8. To stay true to their own values
9. To agree to disagree
10. To ask Residence Life staff for assistance when needed
11. To be treated civilly
12. To be comfortable in their own living space
13. To get their messages in a timely manner
14. To a room free of policy violations

All roommates have the responsibility:

1. To respect each other's privacy
2. To respect themselves and others
3. To communicate openly with their roommate and discuss potential conflicts before they get out of hand
4. To keep their living space neat and clean
5. To lock doors and maintain personal/possession safety
6. To maintain a comfortable environment for sleep and study purposes
7. To treat each other's possessions with care and ask before borrowing personal items
8. To respect differences

9. To compromise

10. To enlist the help of Residence Life staff when a difficult roommate situation arises

11. To be kind and civil with no intent to harm

12. To check with each other before having overnight guests

13. To pass on messages to their roommate in a timely manner

14. To abide by all residence hall rules and regulations

Reprinted with permission from PaperClip Communications. Available at www.paper-clip.com.

6

THE PEOPLE

In high school you probably were with the same people for at least a couple of years. You knew who was who, you had your friends, knew the deal.

Now you're about to be on campus with probably thousands of new people. Maybe a couple you knew before. Or maybe nobody. You have to admit, it's pretty cool to think about the people you're going to meet on campus. Maybe you'll meet a guy from another country or a surfer. You might bump into a DJ, a writer, an activist, a slacker—it takes a diverse mixture of people to put together any college campus. Welcome to the mix.

THE GET-TO-KNOW

So you don't know anyone. Or practically anyone. It's totally natural to feel nervous about meeting new people. But there isn't any big trick to introducing yourself. Remember there are hundreds of other people who don't know anyone at all. Just be yourself, ask questions, be kind. Don't think you have to step into any preordained role. One cool thing about college is that maybe you were shy or a geek in high school. Now you can be anyone you want to be . . . your real self.

The most important thing? Be accepting. You are who you are, and they are who they are. It's not high school where there's one new person and everyone else knows one another. Be nice to your fellow freshmen. The commonality you all share right off the bat is trying to navigate this "dorm thing" together.

You'll eventually be meeting people in class, at the library, at the bars, and other places. But pretty much the first place you'll meet new people is at your dorm.

Ways to Get to Know People on Your Floor

1. Keep your door open when you're around.

2. Organize a group to go to the campus cafeteria or to a restaurant off campus (this might even become a weekly tradition, say, every Sunday night or on theme nights).

3. Invite others to compete against you on your Xbox or PlayStation. Or take this one step further and organize a gaming tournament and invite others to participate—the larger the tournament, the more people who will gain interest and get to know one another.

4. Invite others to participate in a free online fantasy sports league (football in the fall and baseball in the spring).

5. Organize a group to see a comedian or a band, a campus theater production, or some other unique activity around your campus.

6. Be friendly; smile and be accepting of others different from yourself. Whether it's striking up a conversation in the floor/community bathroom or talking to someone in the elevator, make an effort to get to know others.

7. Keep your name tag up on your door and be sure to have a message board.

8. Put up pictures of you and your roommate on your door.

9. Make an effort to have face-to-face and personal connections. Don't rely heavily on technology (IM and e-mail) as a form of communication between you and your roommate or other floormates.

10. Challenge your comfort zone and make an effort to get to know people you might not have class with, participate in athletic events with, or share other common interests with. Don't let space—how the floor/building is set up—dictate your friendships.

—Jeff Kegolis, former assistant director of Residence Life and current assistant professor of psychology at King's College (PA)

CONVERSATION CUES

Wondering how to strike up a conversation with a relative stranger? Look for some simple cues to get you started:

- Dorm bonds: "Did you see if the new menu is up yet?" or "This elevator is taking forever!"
- The team name on their baseball cap or jersey: "So how long have you been a _____ fan?"
- The high school musical, the service project, a 5K run, etc., design on the back of their T-shirt: "Where did you do a Habitat for Humanity build? What was it like?"
- The book they're reading: "I've heard that's a good one. What do you think so far?"
- On the way in to class: "Can I look at your syllabus? I forgot mine."

REMEMBERING NAMES

Think about it. When someone forgets your name, it makes you feel a teeny bit less important. So, why not do unto others as you'd like them to do unto you? Instead of fumbling around when you call Blake "Drake" or Jessica "Jennifer," train your brain with these few simple memory moves:

THE ROUNDABOUT METHOD. A little sneaky action move. If you've completely blanked on somebody's name, say something like "Wait, what's your last name again?" Then look up that person's *full* name in the campus directory or go sneak a peek at door tags. People typically don't mind when you forget their last name. And this is just a way to beat around the bush tactfully to get the complete information you need.

MAKE CONNECTIONS. Use a simple memory device when you meet someone. For instance, when meeting Jean, think of her in blue jeans, or when meeting Trey, think of a dining tray. You know what works for you, so dig into that silly stash for connections that'll trigger something useful.

MEMORY JOGGING. Try to remember where you met someone. This often helps put them in a different context, therefore jogging your memory to the point where their name suddenly comes to you.

REPEAT IT REPEATEDLY. During an initial introduction, be sure to repeat the person's name early in the conversation. This helps solidify it in your mind. And, at the end when you're parting ways, say something like "Nice to meet you, Ben." This plants their name even deeper into your memory.

BELIEVE YOU CAN DO IT! By telling yourself "I can remember names," you're setting yourself up for success.

Saying that you have a poor memory simply becomes a self-fulfilling prophecy because you tend not to put forth as much attention and effort.

FITTING IN

Some people seem to naturally fit in to the dorm right away. Others take their time and then find a fit. For others, it just never really clicks. Speaking of clicks, here's one topic freshmen don't immediately associate with college . . .

CLIQUES

What? Did you think there'd be no cliques in college? You may have left high school and thought it was over for good. No more Jock Guys, Drama People, or Cheerleaders to exclude you, right?

Er, sorry to break it to you, but even in college, cliques can endure. For good or evil, people often bond with people who are like themselves. It could be the cliquey juniors who take over the TV lounge or the frat guys in the dining hall or the college version of the Mean Girls who give you that look when you walk by.

First things first: when you get to school, it can feel safer to latch on to a group of people. You won't have to be alone, you'll know who to sit with in the dining hall. Buuuuuuuuut . . . be careful about jumping in too fast:

- Try not to jump right into an exclusive group for the safety it provides. Make yourself a free agent, interacting with all sorts of people from different walks of life. That's the *difference* between high school and college!

- Get to know people before you clique off. Some fresh-men bond with people only to discover that they're not healthy friendships, or they later meet other people who would be better for them.
- Be careful of people who seem too desperate to have you join them. Okay, people who are lonely still have friendship potential. But, the senior who invites fresh-men girls to *every* meal is just possibly a little desperate for some reason. Something's not quite right—he's ei-ther scamming on you or there's a reason he doesn't have friends his own age.

Some student staff members at King's College (PA) held a "Clique Klatch" roundtable as they reflected on fit-ting in and dealing with the "clique thing." Here are some bits from their conversation that might help you along:

"Cliques aren't necessarily a bad thing," said Kim Fab-bri. "Cliques are usually viewed as negative based on high school experiences, but many college students would agree that, typically, friends that you become close with [in college] are based on your involvement. The group that you become a part of has to do with a common bond or a team mentality."

Sean McLaughlin sees it differently: "Try to avoid cliques. Try to meet as many people as you can. Cliques can be restricting. If you are in a clique, be open-minded and avoid being the textbook definition of a clique, not allowing anyone else into your group of friends."

"Usually people who don't fit in usually aren't as outgo-ing," Trevor Riccobon says, and they're "unwilling to try new things. Therefore, be proactive and make an effort to get to know others." Plus he suggests, "Make an effort to have one good friend. That person can take you to a higher level personally and help you get involved with different things."

Sandra White reassures us, "It's okay to feel like you don't fit in for a while. It's going to take time to find your niche, so be patient and persevere. Realize that others around you might seem very confident in the groups they are in, but keep in mind that they most likely have concerns or nervousness about their adapting to college life as well. Everyone is trying to fit in in some way."

"When you first get to school, it's easy for cliques to form," Allison Ottino recalls. "A lot of times freshmen don't feel like they fit in or have people who they connect with. Don't be afraid to leave the group you originally started with. Don't feel pressured to go with the crowd, either—be your own person and stay true to who you are."

Belonging is a potent force. We're all looking to find a group that embraces us and accepts us for who we are, quirks and all. In college, you're going to find that acceptance in a variety of places, depending on your involvements. You may have a group of coworker friends at your job. Then there may be the group of friends from your dorm whom you eat with and who attend all the hall council meetings with you. You might have a more academic-minded crew in your dorm study group. And you might have your sorority sisters to do social and community service events with. The trick is finding different groups to feed different needs. You won't get everything you need from one small cluster or clique. Branch out and see just how big your campus support system can be.

Don't be disappointed if your first year is somewhat like high school. Eventually the people in the hall who embrace their uniqueness will be embraced back, and those who try to act cooler than they are will have few friends—or join unpopular frats. Oh, and on that note, don't feel pressured to join a frat for the social life, but do join something, anything, martial arts, anime club, whatever!

　　—Paul Lamb, resident advisor at UC Riverside

The friends you make in college while living in the halls can turn out to be the friends you will have for the rest of your life.

　　—George Brelsford, assistant vice president for Student
　　　Affairs and dean of students at Rowan University (NJ)

Keep your door open. Almost everyone in your dorm wants to make friends, and there's no better invitation than an open door.

　　—David Terraso, media relations specialist with Institute
　　　Communications and Public Affairs, Georgia Tech

Be nice to those around you. You never know when they may be interviewing you for a job or even may be your boss in the future.

　　—Eric Galdi, resident assistant at University of Wisconsin,
　　　Platteville

Reinvent yourself! This is the time to break out of the mold you've been put in for the last 18 years. Challenge yourself to be the person you really want to be.

　　—Sarah Scott Hall, director of Residence Life and
　　　Counseling at Centre College (KY)

NOT FITTING IN

Sometimes you'll end up in a dorm and feel out of place. Other people will naturally fit in and will immediately seem to be having fun and relaxing. You'll feel weird entering the TV lounge or you'll worry the fun is going on without you. You won't feel at home.

Not ideal. But not abnormal, either. Sometimes it might seem like if you don't fit in with others in your dorm, you won't fit in at college at all. But remember that your dorm is just one tiny part of the college. Just because your dorm experience sucks does NOT mean your entire college experience will suck. Think of it like this. You expect to have a bad professor or a bad class sometimes; well, some people have bad dorm life. And don't think you're a bad person. Even if everyone is having fun around you in your dorm, eh, oh well. They found a fit and you didn't; doesn't mean anything is wrong with you. You may just have had the bad luck to enter a cliquey, boring, or just plain unfriendly group of people.

If you've tried to be friendly and involved and it doesn't happen, let it go. Move on. Literally! Change dorms to find one with a "personality" that fits you better. And sooner or later you might be able to move off campus. But in the meantime, find outside activities, clubs, or classes where you feel that you're more a part of the scene. Don't give up or be depressed. Keep looking, and you'll find a place that is you.

THE DORM DATING SCENE

Ah, dorm romance—the dormance. When you throw lots of college students into one coed living space, well, sparks can fly. The cute guy in the elevator, the hot girl in the TV lounge. It's all very convenient. I mean, it's way easy to "accidentally" walk by the object of your affection's room on the way to the dining hall. Depending on the dorm, in-dorm dating can be normal or can seem incestuous; it can be long lasting, or it can be really disruptive.

. . . .

You can tell you're a freshman if you . . .
- carry a purse around during the first few weeks
- get dressed up for class
- use a map to navigate your way around
- aren't sure what all the campus acronyms and lingo mean
- live with at least one or two other people in a squishy space

You can tell you're a sophomore if you . . .
- live in the dorm that you chose
- frequently wear sweatpants and baseball caps
- are trying to figure out your major
- feel more comfortable with speaking up in class and expressing your opinion
- have all the important phone numbers memorized, from Public Safety to Domino's

You can tell you're a junior if you . . .
- like to just hang out with a core group of good friends
- are looking for a meaningful summer job or internship
- live in upperclass housing, like suites or apartments
- have occasional I-graduate-next-year freak-out moments
- question whether you're studying the right thing

You can tell you're a senior if you . . .
- are getting some credits for doing an internship or independent study
- have increasing I-graduate-this-year freak-out moments
- live off-campus or in upperclass housing
- spend an awful lot of time in Career Services
- get hit by waves of nostalgia at the most unexpected times

I've seen the good and the bad. My own freshman roommate (after I escaped the triple and no longer had to fall off the top bunk) met a guy on our floor, and they're now married and have two kids. But another girl in my dorm left the dorm after her hookup with the guy down the hall turned into a creepy stalker situation.

With all these romance possibilities, what's the smart thing to do? Should you date someone whom you're in a living situation with? John Palmer, a residence director at the University of Wisconsin, Whitewater, has an opinion on that one: "I suggest not dating on the same floor in coed buildings," he says. "This can cause many problems for the community."

If you *do* choose to hook up with someone in your community, though, keep the following tips in mind:

BEWARE OF LECHEROUS LOTHARIOS. There will always be upperclass students who seem charming and mature but who are really preying on new students, maybe even in a contest with others to see who can score the most. While most RAs and orientation guides really are there to help you, others have different intentions (like checking out the fresh meat first). Don't get hooked into their scheme.

GUARD YOUR REPUTATION. People really do gossip about the floor sluts—guys and girls. It's not pretty. And in-dorm hookups make the best gossip, because you know a lot of the same people. Making smart choices about alcohol and other drugs has many benefits, including the fact that, when you're in control of yourself, you can also control your reputation. Choose to get sloppy drunk and make out with the RA in the laundry room and, chances are, it might be hard to show your face at brunch the next morning.

BE CAREFUL IN ROOMS. Just because you live in the same dorm with someone doesn't mean you should automatically trust them and choose to be alone with them in their room right off the bat. So if you're not totally comfortable or sure about visiting that guy you're crushing on, bring a friend. That's perfectly acceptable in the dorms; people are always going in and out of one another's rooms like that.

TOO MUCH OF A GOOD THING? How good is it to spend *all* of your time with the person you're dating? After all, you're still meeting new people and figuring things out! If you choose to hole up with your love muffin all the time, you'll be shutting out the other people and possibilities in your life. Plus, your roommate will have *every right* to be ticked off if your new hottie has practically moved in.

BE PREPARED FOR FALLOUT. Dating someone in the dorm can be a recipe for disaster, no doubt. Two words: bad breakup. If, after a whirlwind month of dating, you get dumped, you'll still have to see this person day in and day out. It might be totally awkward and totally traumatic. You'll have to watch them go out with other people. Just keep this in mind if you decide to go for a dormance.

WATCH OUT FOR THE RA-MANCE. While your RA may be adorable and smart, and they might make you feel important, don't confuse an RA's interest in you with Interest. It's the RA's *job* to check in, to make sure you are doing okay, and to involve you socially in the programs they host and with other residents. Especially in first-year halls, crushes on RAs are common. And why not? You have a fantastic senior guy knocking on your door. But he's knocking on *everybody else's* door, too. Besides, RAs aren't really supposed to date their residents (policies differ depending on the school). Regardless of the official policy, RA-resident dating is always highly discouraged, despite what you saw on *Felicity!*

DORM DATING DO'S

So you've decided you don't care about the consequences and want to go for the neighbor nookie. Here's how to make the most of dorm dating life:

1. Start things off right. The best time to meet people is on move-in day and during the first week of school. This is the time when *everyone* is introducing themselves to everybody else, so don't be shy during this time. If you see someone interesting, say hi (really, don't be afraid) and make move-in an opportunity to help someone in need ("Can I help you carry that box?"). Strike up a conversation, *and* find a reason to see them again ("Hey, if I come back later with a pen, will you tell me where you got that great lamp?").

2. Go to every dorm activity you can, whether it's movie night in the lounge or a night out on the town. It's a great way to meet people in a nonparty environment and often provides a better setting for conversation. Also, know that as a resident, you can even suggest programs to your RA that might be of interest to you and to others in your hall. Your RA has a budget to spend on just the kind of get-to-know-you events that you have in mind for meeting that interesting theater major who can't resist free tickets to a play.

3. Set your roommates up. Suggest a blind-date dance if your residence hall or college doesn't already have one (lots do). They are fun and are great ways to meet people you'd otherwise never have the guts to say hello to. Here's why: your roommates do all the work. You and your roommate(s) set each other up on a blind date, and you all meet for the first time the night of the dance. It is not uncommon for roommates to give each other long lists of "possibilities" (i.e., people you'd like to see show up at your door the night of the dance). Then each of you goes on a quest to get each other a date. It's the perfect way to meet who you want, without any of the stress.

4. Remember, there *are* other floors in your hall; don't be limited by geography. You might not find the perfect match down the hall, but they might just be living upstairs on the seventh floor! Here is where knowing your RA can be helpful, too: RAs all hang out together and are often expected to do events with one another. Find out who Ms. Perfect's RA is, and then suggest that your RA host a program with her RA. Depending on how comfortable you are talking with your RA, you can even suggest a little matchmaking on their part, to ensure

that your girl shows up at the event. RAs often like to set up their residents and sometimes even scheme to make this happen on their own.

5. Another great way to get to know a really interesting crowd is to apply to be an RA yourself. You can be of service to the community and become part of a new community yourself. As far as dating goes, I am *not* saying that RAs should date each other; in fact, dating the other RAs who work in your hall is usually discouraged. But, especially at larger universities where there are often hundreds of RAs, it is not uncommon to find love across campus on someone else's staff! At the very least, it's a way to meet some cool people you missed out on during your first year of college.

Some information in the last two sections contributed by Donna Freitas, PhD, author of *Becoming a Goddess of Inner Poise* and *Save the Date,* professor at St. Michael's College (VT), and former Residence Life staff at New York University

- -

BAD DORM HOOKUP LINES

- Wanna come help me test how strong my loft is?
- Can I buy you dinner—on my meal card?
- So my roommate is going out of town this weekend . . .

- -

THE DIFFERENCE MADE BY DIFFERENCE

You'll be exposed to new ideas, new perspectives, and new ways of doing things while living in your community.

You'll be exposed to different cultures, religions, abilities, sexual orientations, races, sizes, genders; basically, you'll be exposed to *difference*. So:

- Expand beyond your comfort zone
- Talk with people from different backgrounds
- Listen to different ways of thinking
- Be challenged and inspired by your peers
- Show an interest in different cultures and ways of life

When you find yourself surrounded by difference, it can be overwhelming. You get the sense that you don't even know how much you have to learn. And that can leave you wondering where to begin. First step: have an open mind.

"Admit that there's a lot you *don't* know," encourages Tomás Gonzalez, the assistant director of Residence Life for Diversity Initiatives at Syracuse University (NY). "We all have biases and it's okay . . . it's a matter of what we *do* with them."

For instance, if you tell a biased joke and then say, "I didn't *mean* anything by it," where does that leave things? Are you making an excuse? Are you saying that you won't tell that biased joke again? Or are you failing to see your role in perpetuating a bias?

Tomás knows that many students come to college and quickly recognize that "their frame of reference isn't like everybody else's." That's why he says, "To be successful at school and beyond that, you need to recognize your biases." Be willing to ask questions and don't shut down over fear that you'll say "the wrong thing." Instead, Tomás suggests, admit that "this is what I know, but it's not everything." And then think about ways you can strengthen your relationships with people who are different from you. Here are a few simple things to get you started:

- Ask other students what holidays they celebrate and what some of their special traditions are.

- If someone has an unusual name that you haven't heard before, ask them what it means.

- When someone tells you that they grew up in _____, ask them what it was like to live there.

- If someone is cooking in the common area kitchen, ask what recipe they're using.

- Don't walk on eggshells—ask direct questions as long as you have a genuine interest in the answers.

- Attend different cultural programs, lectures, and festivals to expand your horizons.

- Ask someone who speaks a different language to teach you a few keywords and phrases.

Expanding beyond your comfort zone is incredibly worthwhile because you'll connect with someone different and likely learn something in the process. After college, as our world continues to become more and more diverse, the ability and the willingness to embrace difference will be the marker between life success and failure.

Is everyone politically correct? Nope. Are there close-minded people in college who don't really care if they offend others? Yep. But you don't have to be one of them, and just one person can make a big difference.

While living in a residence hall, I was exposed to such great diversity that I never experienced before. I met people from different cultures and backgrounds. I met people who didn't think like me and who grew up in a totally different atmosphere. At first, this scared me. But, living

*in a residence hall gives you great opportunities to meet
people . . . I think it was a comfortable way to expand my
horizons and give me the courage to leap to other things.
I also met people who challenged me—friends who were
studying abroad—and I talked to them before and after.
I never felt I had the courage to live abroad, but I guess
I do, as I moved to Japan for two years to teach English.*

—Rebecca Parillo, director of Study Abroad at Ashland
University (OH), referring to her undergrad years at St.
Michael's College (VT)

BEING INCLUSIVE

Inclusive communities are ones where people go out of
their way to welcome one another, quirks, differences,
and all. Does that sound like the type of community you'd
like to live in? If so, there are a few easy things you can do
to help foster that inclusive feel:

- Don't assume that everyone has the type of family structure that you do. Some people are raised by their
  grandparents, others are from single-parent house-
  holds, some have guardians, others have two or more
  parents. Using the term *your family* instead of *your parents* can be more inclusive as it embraces a variety of
  family situations.
- Don't assume that all relationships are heterosexual. If
  you ask that guy down the hall whether he has a girlfriend, you could unwittingly be driving him deeper
  into the closet if he really has a boyfriend he's too
  scared to tell people about. Figure out a term that feels
  comfortable to you, whether it's *significant other* or
  something else, that includes different kinds of relationships. Or just ask, "Are you going out with anyone?"

- Don't assume that everyone celebrates the same holidays or practices the same religion. See how it feels to say "Happy Holidays" in December rather than just "Happy Hanukkah" or "Merry Christmas." Sometimes those simple things can make a world of difference.
- Make sure your language isn't harmful. Saying things like "It's ghetto" or "That's so retarded" may cause some students to feel excluded or offended—and uncomfortable with you. So think twice before speaking!
- Don't pigeonhole males and females into specific categories (i.e., women want to talk about feelings but men do not, only the males will be interested in the late-night basketball game, etc.).
- Don't make fun of particular groups or individuals in the quest to be funny. Maybe that Polish joke can be just as funny without humiliating anyone (or just substitute people from your rival school instead).
- Don't try to speak to someone in the way they speak if it's not your natural style. They might think you're trying too hard or even making fun of them. If you don't usually talk street, they'll know it.

Being inclusive isn't always easy, and you might stumble along the way. That's okay. If your intention is to help create a community where all folks feel welcomed, people will understand where you're coming from.

As a foreign student who had lived in the University of Maryland residence halls throughout my entire four-year degree, I was no stranger to the notion of feeling like an outsider. When I first arrived from Australia and was thrust almost immediately into a hall full of American

freshmen, it took a really long time to feel at home. So,
when I became an RA, I was determined to have a presence
on the floor that would show the residents that I cared.
I also made every attempt to get to know ALL of my
residents, not just the ones that I got along with the best.
I realize this is all very basic stuff that we hear over and
over again . . . but it simply is true. The best sense of
community stems from an environment of inclusiveness.

—Dale Barltrop, a former University of Maryland, College
Park, student/RA from Australia

NONTRADITIONAL STUDENTS

Graduate students, married students, older returning
students—some live off campus but some do actually live
in dorms. If you're a nontraditional student looking for a
social life, then a dorm may be a great place for you to
live; cheaper and more convenient. Many schools offer
graduate dorms tailored just for grad students or married
students. Other times, you're mixed in with everyone else.
If you're coming to graduate school with the intention of
working hard and focusing primarily on your work with
few interruptions, then an apartment off campus may
work better.

If you're living near a nontraditional student, be open
to learning from them. Instead of just thinking of them as
the resident grown-up to ignore, ask them about their
work experiences, their life experiences. It's a heads-up of
what's to come for you.

I went into graduate school as a single woman having been
in the work world for two years postcollege, so I was still
young and looking to meet new friends. My closest friends
during my two years in graduate school were from the dorm.

I met people from around the country and the world who were studying and doing research in a wide variety of areas. Living in the dorm gave me access to these people that I wouldn't have had if I lived on my own off campus and just met people through my own graduate program. Having the meal plan gave me a great opportunity to get to know people and to relax after a busy day of classes.

—Deborah Wachenheim, former grad student in the dorms of Harvard University (MA)

SERVICES FOR STUDENTS WITH SPECIAL NEEDS

Residence halls may offer a variety of services for people with special needs. Ask if your dorm has

- flashing strobe lights, smoke detectors/fire alarms, and bed-shaker devices for deaf or hard-of-hearing students
- large-print student handbooks and other documents for students with visual impairments
- accessible rooms on first floors for students in wheelchairs
- special elevators with keycode or card access for students with mobility issues
- air-conditioned rooms for students with asthma

GLBTQ STUDENTS

As a student who is gay, lesbian, bisexual, transgender, or questioning (GLBTQ), you may be wondering how you fit in to the whole "dorm thing." Well, dorm life is for everyone. And that includes you. You have every right to feel comfortable where you live. So, whether you've come out or not, make the dorm your home.

And keep in mind that your residence hall staff members are trained extensively on creating welcoming, open environments. They are taught about GLBTQ issues, so they can support you and lend a hand if you run into any troubles, too. Call on them if you run into roommate problems, harassment, or threats. Your RA and your hall director are allies.

Some schools, such as Wesleyan University (CT) and the University of California, Riverside, are making transgender floors available to students. There are all kinds of living arrangements available—find the one that fits you best.

WHY SHOULD I CARE?

Because . . .

- ALL people deserve to be welcomed and drawn into the campus fold, not just you.
- Your way is not the only way.
- Interacting with someone who is different from you almost always results in a good learning experience.
- When you stretch outside of your comfort zone, you grow as a person.
- Life would be boring without difference!

The hall community represents the real world, an incubator of diversity, thriving with people from an array of different backgrounds, experiences, and perspectives.

Living in this kind of community is a great preparation for the real world.

—Elizabeth Costello, RA at East Carolina University (NC)

If you have a positive attitude and look for the opportunities to get involved, make a difference, and open your mind, you will be successful, and people will want to be around you. Everyone likes a positive person that can always be counted on to come through during crunch times. Are you going to be that person?

—James "JJ" Manley, the assistant director of Residential Services at the State University of New York College at Cortland

THE RESIDENCE HALL STAFF

Some key staff members make the halls an exciting, educational, and enlightening place to be. They also help to keep you safe and secure. And all the while they also try to help you be the best version of yourself possible.

YOUR RA (RESIDENT ASSISTANT)

RAs. Some schools call them CAs (Community Advisors), SAs (Student Assistants), or any number of other titles, but they're the student leaders who live in the hall and are ultimately responsible for helping to build and maintain the community in which you will live. The RA plays a number of roles in the residence hall. (S)he can serve as a friend, a resource, a mentor, an event planner, a role model, and a community leader.

—Daniel P. Oltersdorf, former RA at Colorado State, coauthor of *Inspiration for RAs* and *Inspiration for Student Leaders,* and founder of the website www.ResidentAssistant.com

RAs differ as much as the general population of students. Some RAs are good listeners, others are more into talking. Some are quiet, some are outgoing. Some are well-trained and great at solving problems. Others just aren't emotionally equipped to handle a lot of residents' problems. Some are objective and professional. Some hook up with their residents. It's hit or miss. You might hang with your RA, look up to your RA, or not ever see your RA.

Why do students become RAs?

- They want to help other students thrive in the dorms.
- They had an RA role model and they wanted to be like them.
- They had a lame RA and thought, "I can do better."
- They needed the money and free room and board.
- They're teacher types, into planning and running programs and activities.
- They're power-hungry and want to order people around.
- They're lonely and think it's a way to make new friends.
- They're natural leaders, and the job is a good fit.
- They think it will look good on their résumé.
- They think it seems fun.

Or any combo of those.

But however it shakes out, remember that your RA can be one of the greatest resources you have on campus. Seriously. Remember that your RA is also a student who has already "been there, done that" and can serve as a great source of information and advice. And yeah, while your RA is still a student and may not have all the answers, she is extensively trained to know the resources available on and off campus.

Your RA will likely plan various programs and activities on your floor and in your building. Your RA wants these programs to be fun and successful, so let him know what you are interested in and what activities you would like to see. Activities vary widely and could include social events like bowling and pizza, educational events such as a workshop on how to choose a major, or cultural events like an international food potluck. The goal of all of these events goes back to making your residence hall a great place to live and grow as a person and as a student. Attend these events whenever possible. Why?

- These events are the best way to get to know the other people in your community, particularly early in the year.
- Many of the programs are educational and provide excellent learning opportunities.
- They provide the chance for you to connect with faculty and staff members.

Sometimes the RA is seen by residents as "the cop" on the floor. The RA might be subject to taunts, abuse, and pissed-off students who get themselves in trouble. While it's true that policy enforcement is part of the RA job description, it's not the main part of the job. If your RA lets you know you have violated a policy or asks you to turn your music down, don't take it personally! Remember that your RA is a student just like you, and they're just doing their job.

For most RAs, it's not about a hierarchy or "busting" fellow students when they go astray. Yeah, that's a necessary part of the position, primarily so you will make better choices and stay safe in the meantime. Most RAs, though, apply for the position because they want to work with students in positive ways, building a strong floor community while getting to know individual residents, one person at a time.

FAMOUS RAS!

Check out the people who served as RAs during their college years:

- Katie Couric of the *Today Show* at the University of Virginia
- Actor Jerry O'Connell of *Crossing Jordan* at New York University
- Comedian Paul Reiser *(Mad About You)* at Binghamton University (NY)
- Singer/songwriter Sheryl Crow at the University of Missouri at Columbia
- Actor Wesley Snipes *(Blade)* at the State University of New York at Purchase
- U.S. Senator Hillary Rodham Clinton at Wellesley College (MA)
- Coach Mike Ditka at the University of Pittsburgh (PA)
- Meg Cabot, author of *Princess Diaries,* at NYU (assistant dorm manager)

RAs are not stupid. They were once normal students just like everyone else. They know that when you have a hard, rectangle backpack late on a Saturday night, you are probably not going to the library. A case of beer has a very different look than a bunch of books.

—Jill Yashinsky, assistant hall director at St. Norbert College (WI)

YOUR HALL DIRECTOR

Another key staff member who lives in the residence hall with you is your hall director (HD). They used to be called "house mothers" or "dorm counselors." Today, though, this person is likely a full-time professional with a bachelor's or master's degree, often in a field like counseling, human resources, college student personnel, or higher education administration. No matter their background, one thing remains consistent: HDs have *chosen* to live where they work because they want to create the best possible living environment for students. Their concerns range from basic housing needs to the educational, emotional, academic, and health needs of the students. They love working with college students and getting to know them. Being an HD can be a tough, but very rewarding, job.

WHAT DO HALL DIRECTORS DO?

When you see your HD racing from one thing to another, it's because of all the in-hall, departmental, and all-campus responsibilities this person has that take place throughout campus. For instance, an HD

- supervises the RAs
- advises hall government
- coordinates faculty involvement initiatives in the residence halls
- offers academic assistance and informal career counseling
- counsels students on everything from concerns about classes to homesickness (and everything in between)
- encourages and plans educational programs
- refers students to appropriate resources
- runs staff meetings and staff development activities

- supervises other dorm staff, such as assistant hall directors, RAs, desk staff, and support staff
- works closely with the cleaning and maintenance staff
- handles housing assignments/switches
- mediates conflicts
- holds office hours
- administers assessment tools to make sure students are getting the most out of dorm life
- hears judicial cases such as minor alcohol violations, noise complaints, or vandalism situations
- advises other student organizations outside of the dorm
- works with all-campus leadership initiatives
- coordinates all sorts of special projects, from Wellness Week to technology surveys
- might attend classes

Hall directors keep you safe, manage your environment, and challenge you to take leadership positions. They also challenge you to take more responsibility for your own behavior, to apply for staff jobs, to strive to do better academically, and to get to know someone different from yourself. When it's about reaching your potential and becoming the best version of yourself possible, HDs are there, often behind the scenes, rooting you on. And in an atmosphere where you may sometimes feel like just a number, Dr. Jodi Lambdin Devine, associate director of Academic Affairs for the University Honors Program at Bowling Green State University (OH), says, "Hall directors are the people who don't know you as a number. They go beyond that."

Jodi describes how HDs can benefit students:

- They are invaluable career resources.
- They can be great role models.
- They are there to help with your problems.
- They help you see multiple sides of things.
- They know how to network.
- They have expertise.
- They can talk about the tough issues.

BEHIND THE SCENES: OTHER KEY STAFFERS IN THE DORMS

- *Desk staff/attendants.* These student workers staff the front desk, doing everything from answering phones to sorting mail to handing out equipment—and so much more.
- *Night clerks/night security.* They are the ones checking students and guests in after desk hours, making sure doors aren't propped open, and providing for your safety.
- *Computer lab workers.* If your hall has a computer lab, these student techies can help with those technology problems.
- *Support staff.* Sometimes, depending on the size of your community, there will be a professional support person who works behind the scenes with your HD to make sure things run smoothly.
- *Faculty fellows.* Some halls have faculty living in a dorm apartment, and others have faculty who are connected to the hall. This professor or instructor is there for advising, running programs, and informal interaction.
- *Community police officers.* You may have one or a few Public Safety officers assigned to your dorm, so get to know them before any problems arise. They can be very important people to know!

- *Hall council execs.* These are the students in your hall who serve in executive leadership positions within hall government, working for students and getting things done.
- *Cleaning crew.* In some dorms, cleaning people will actually clean your room, but in most dorms they only clean the common areas. They have a hard enough job cleaning up after you—don't *expect* them to clean your messes. Clean up after yourself and be friendly! Remember, they have been around longer than you, so treat them with respect, and they might reciprocate by sharing some of their wisdom about the school or the community.

SPIRITUAL ADVISORS

Pepperdine University's (CA) "spiritual life advisors" are students who live in the residence halls and serve in a ministry that provides "soul care" for other students. SLA volunteers serve as the chaplain to students by fostering an atmosphere that encourages spiritual growth through building relationships and being involved with the residents, showing concern for them by listening and praying with them, and being available to residents for individual ministry.

7

LIVING IN YOUR COMMUNITY

GETTING USED TO THE DORMS

I've already said it, and I'll say it again. Living in a dorm is, in many ways, not normal. It takes some adjusting. And everyone adjusts in their own way.

It's normal to feel lonely the first few weeks, or even longer. Some students look around them and think that everyone is fitting in so much better than they are. In some cases, it's true. Some students take to the dorms naturally and are socially successful. Other students start off feeling confident, but when the honeymoon period wears off, they suddenly feel out of it. Other students are uncomfortable for a while, but then slowly feel like they fit in. Others are on an emotional rollercoaster where some days they love it, other days they don't. Adjusting to the dorms is different for everyone.

But everyone has *some* adjusting to do. So you're not alone.

One of the keys to getting used to—and enjoying—the dorms is to appreciate and take advantage of what's around you. Sure, maybe your room is cramped. Your roommate is getting on your nerves. Sharing a bathroom is crazy. But hold on—take a minute to appreciate dorm life.

You'll make friendships that will last far beyond your college years, have immediate access to great resources and technology, not have to worry about finding a parking spot before class starts, and most important, you will know the phone number to every local pizza place by heart. Besides, it sure beats having to do the dishes and mow the lawn at your parents' house if you were still living there while getting your college education.

 —Kyle O'Dell, assistant director of Residence Life at John Carroll University (OH)

Totally true.

Your Dorm's Personality

Your dorm kind of has a personality. Take this quiz to find out what it is.

1. Which shoe best "fits" your hall/floor style?
 a. Sneakers: comfortable, sporty
 b. Strappy heels: always up for a party
 c. Flip-flops: ultra-casual, hanging out
 d. Sandals: outdoorsy and adventurous
 e. Sensible shoes: maybe not stylish, but comfy
 f. Barefoot: very homey and down-to-earth

2. If a movie or TV show were made about your floor/hall, what would it be?
 a. Comedy
 b. Drama
 c. Reality show
 d. Business channel show
 e. Horror movie
 f. Chick flick

3. Okay, so in this movie, who plays your dorm?
   a. Jennifer Aniston: cool, laid-back, funny
   b. Ben Stiller: outrageous, hilarious
   c. Oprah Winfrey: compassionate, philanthropic
   d. Jessica Simpson: bubbly and silly
   e. Adam Brody: kinda nerdy but cool
   f. Britney Spears: careful, may be spinning out of control!

4. Which food is your floor/hall most like?
   a. Apple pie: wholesome, dependable, friendly
   b. Salsa: spicy, hot!
   c. Power bar: energizing, on the go
   d. Wheat cracker: bland
   e. Party mix: always up for a good time

Okay, there's no answer section (you get the idea, anyway). The point is to get you thinking about your dorm's personality. And now, think about your personality. Is it compatible with your dorm's? If it isn't, that's fine. You just haven't found the right fit for you or maybe you should try to strike up a conversation with someone else who doesn't seem to gel with the rest of the dorm's image. Take these factors into consideration when you're moving to your next home.

THE RIGHT FIT

But even if the dorm's personality doesn't fit, and you're not totally comfortable yet, it doesn't mean you still can't enjoy a lot of the benefits of living there. The key is to focus on the positive. If your roommate issues are bum-

REAL WORLD: ADJUSTING

"I was immediately comfortable in the dorms—too comfortable. I found a boyfriend on my floor the first week, I made insta-best friends. Everything was awesome. For about a month. Then the boyfriend and I broke up. My new best friends turned out to be backstabbers. My roommate got tired of me having people in our room all the time and we started fighting. The rest of the semester was downhill, and it took me a little while to find my true place."

   —Andrea, American University (DC)

"I felt really alone for the first two months. I saw all these people bonding and having a great time and I thought there must be something wrong with me. At first I just played video games in my room all the time. Then I went to the game room and started playing there, and this guy challenged me to a game. We ended up becoming roommates the next quarter."

   —Evan, Bradley University (IL)

"At first I was overwhelmed, but I took some time checking things out. I didn't jump into any relationships, but I tried to be friendly. And I ended up having a great time in my hall."

   —Ashley, Washington State

ming you out, then focus on the fact that there's a girl who likes to go to the movies with you who lives one floor up. If you're feeling cramped in your small room, focus on the joy of having a fitness center right downstairs. If you're feeling lonely and like you don't fit in, focus on your studying and that maybe your grades will be the best ever this semester—and next year when you're in another dorm, you'll have the year of your social life.

That's another key—life in the dorms is temporary. You only live there for a year or two or four, so focus on the positive. If you haven't found the positive yet, read on and see what your dorm has to offer that you might have been missing.

DORM FACILITIES

Okay, here's the part that you want to read really well so you take advantage of all this stuff. Because you may never ever again have the opportunity to live in a place that has everything that a residence hall offers. When you move to an apartment, you definitely won't have all this. If you get married and move to the suburbs, you'll have more living space, but you probably won't have all these amenities in your home. Not even hotels offer all the extras you get in the dorms. For example, you could enjoy:

- A fitness facility
- Pool tables, foosball, and Ping-Pong tables
- A computer lab
- A TV lounge
- Free video checkouts and/or access to a channel that runs new movies
- Vending machines

- A kitchen
- Laundry machines
- Games and sports equipment for loan
- Bike parking
- Classrooms
- A recycling center
- A study center or writing lab

WANT MORE?

What? No pool table? TV too small? Lots of dorms have incentive programs that can help you earn more good stuff for community use. For instance, if your floor has no vandalism all semester, you may be rewarded with some new furniture. Or, if you have the best hall government attendance all month, maybe you can win a new TV for your lounge. Check into what's available by talking with your Residence Life staffers.

Another way to add on some amenities is through involvement with hall government. Would you like to see a CD burner added to the computer lab or have a juice machine installed? Go to hall government with a well-thought-out proposal. You may be asked to chair a fund-raising initiative to help pay for the new stuff, but it's all possible! You'll be amazed at what you can get.

Take advantage of your dorm resources. If you're lonely, practice becoming a pool shark. If you're stressed, hit the workout room. If you're bored, rent a free movie or try a new board game . . . or . . . or . . .

THE FRONT DESK

One of the best-kept secrets is the front desk. Think of it as a concierge at a hotel. Okay, maybe not exactly like a hotel. They likely won't offer wake-up calls or replace your dirty towels. But want to pick up a package? Go to the front desk. Want to borrow a video or DVD? Chances are the front desk can help. Need a number for a local taxi company? Front desk. Or if you're just looking for someone to talk with during that all-nighter, the student worker at the twenty-four-hour desk may be dying for company to help keep him awake.

THE FACTS ABOUT FLOOR MEETINGS

Ready to blow off the floor meeting? I mean, it seems like there are better things to do with your time—sleep, go to a party, sleep . . . Plus, aren't floor meetings kinda dorky?

Maybe . . . but maybe not. Actually that's a big maybe not, especially at the first couple meetings. Attending those floor meetings is a simple way to stay in the loop, especially in the beginning of the year. "It's important to attend meetings," stresses Susan Ratz-Thomas, the assistant dean of Student Life and coordinator of Judicial Affairs at Southern Methodist University (TX). "The opportunity to meet new people is key."

And floor meetings can be pretty fun. Your RA might throw in an icebreaker so you can get to know your fellow floormates better. And there's often free pizza! Free snacks! Plus, you can scope out the other people on your floor and share information. Floor meetings are also a forum where you can bring up community issues and try to solve them peacefully. If you've got questions or issues about your social life, the living conditions, whatever, talk to your roommates or floor friends in advance. And then bring up the issues in the meeting. Floor meetings are for you, so make the best of them. In a twenty-minute span of time, you can find out what's going on in your hall and on campus. It's relatively painless, and the payoffs really do outweigh the extra twenty minutes of naptime you might lose.

TREAT YOUR DORM RIGHT

There's one sure way to be disliked by your dormmates and staff and that's by trashing shared spaces and equipment. Be respectful of those special amenities or else suffer the consequences. You'll likely be fined.

> *We used to have ice machines but we don't anymore because too many people peed in them.*
>
> —Troy Moldenhauer, assistant director of Admissions at University of Wisconsin, Whitewater

Residence hall staff give these additional reports:

- If you decide to toss a study room table down the stairwell in a late-night fit of the stupids, your fellow residents won't have an adequate place to study. They'll be pissed off.
- If you pry open the elevator doors and they don't go back to normal, your whole building might be charged for the damage. Don't fess up and you'll be disliked immensely!
- If you and your friends make furniture sculptures in the lounge, a floormate might climb on top and fall.

- If you damage the vending machine in a "Give-me-my-Doritos-dammit!" frenzy, no one else will be able to get their late-night munchie fix. Hungry people are cranky people!
- If you think shooting off fire extinguishers is fun, you're putting your friends and peers in danger. What if an extinguisher is empty when it's *really* needed?

COMMON AREA ETIQUETTE (AKA, HOW TO MAKE SURE OTHERS DON'T HATE YOU)

Treat common areas like they're your home and return things to where they were. The cleaner everyone keeps the area and the more responsible people are with it, the better it is to live in that specific community.

—John Palmer, a residence director at the University of Wisconsin, Whitewater

Here are some simple ways to treat common spaces with respect:

- Don't leave gobs of toothpaste in the bathroom sinks—that's just gross.
- Don't hold the elevators so long that the buzzer goes off—especially late at night.
- Don't leave spills in the stairwells—someone could slip and get really hurt.
- Don't hog the lounge TV—your obsession with *Judge Judy* doesn't mean others want her on all the time.
- Don't leave the common kitchen a wreck after you bake cookies—old, wet flour gets downright slimy.
- Don't dump your stinky garbage in the common lounge—just take it down to the Dumpster.
- Don't leave half-eaten sandwiches and sticky stuff in the study rooms—your floor will get bugs.

- Don't expect that others will clean up after you.

Please don't open your windows while the air-conditioning is on. This creates the perfect environment for the growth of mold, and trust me, you don't want that!

    —Joanne M. Black, assistant director of Student Services at the Washington Center for Internships and Academic Seminars, Washington, D.C.

DORM LIFE IN THE MEDIA

- TV's Felicity did *not* cut her hair just because she fell for her RA and then got into a complex love triangle with Ben and Noel. Maybe she just wanted a shorter do so she could take quicker showers in the dorm bathroom! Ever think of that?!
- *Animal House* is NOT an accurate depiction of dorm life. Neither is *Old School.* (Although having Will Ferrell on campus would probably be a riot, don't you think?)
- The *Gilmore Girls'* Rory had her best friend live with her for a while in her Yale dorm room, even though she wasn't going to school there. Yeah, not a good idea. It's against a whole *lot* of rules.
- And how did members of the *Dawson's Creek* gang manage to all go to college near one another? Silly, codependent bunch.

When I would find discarded pizza boxes left in the lounge or hall, I would leave the student a package slip [in his or her mailbox]. The student would be so excited to be receiving a package, that when she realized her package was just her pizza box from the night before, it made her rethink leaving her trash for someone else to pick up.

> —Kara Lombardi, associate director of the Career Center at Duke University (NC) and a former Residence Life professional

DORM RULES

Yeah, it's sometimes fun to bend the rules and see what you can get away with. Even Dr. Seuss did that during his Dartmouth years. That's right, he and some friends had a party "that did not coincide with school policy," and he was consequently removed as editor in chief of the school's humor magazine. That's when the student formerly known as Ted Geisel started signing his work "Seuss" (his middle name), so he could still sneak in some submissions. Funny to think that the Dr. Seuss name came about because of a party gone wrong!

But this also shows that there are consequences to breaking the rules. The same holds true for today's residence halls. Just remember that the policies and procedures for your dorm are in place to keep you safe and sound, not to make your life unbearably miserable!

One thing about dorm life: you will LOVE your freedom. No one is going to babysit you and make sure you are home and get enough sleep at night. Just remember that going out until 3:00 A.M. six nights a week gets real old real fast. You want to enjoy the luxury of freedom, so don't abuse it. You can reach burnout in a matter of weeks . . . some

manage to make it there by the end of their first week.
Don't let that be you.

—Ashey Theres, community advisor at Alverno College (WI)

I GOT BUSTED!

How can you keep from uttering those famous last words? After talking to hundreds of college students who have found themselves on the wrong side of the law, I've learned some things you should know, both before and after you find yourself uttering, "I got busted!"

WHEN YOU FIRST GET TO CAMPUS

Living in the dorms is your first real taste of freedom. You make your own decisions. Which also means when things go wrong, it's all about you. So . . .

- *Go to your floor meetings.* This is where you become more than a name in a room to your RA. It is also where your RA shares with you some of the most commonly violated rules in the residence halls.
- *Read your handbook.* There's a reason it is given to you. You should know the general rights and responsibilities for your campus, not to mention knowing the rules and policies.
- *Ask questions.* If you think it might be against the rules—and this is where common sense comes in—it probably is. But when in doubt, ask your RA *before* you do it!

NOW YOU'VE DONE IT . . .

Well, it happened. You did something that was against all those rules that you were supposed to have read. How should you proceed now?

- *Don't hate the RA who busted you.* They're hired to do a job, and it's usually nothing personal. If they don't do their job, they can get fired.
- *Don't claim ignorance.* You probably knew you were doing something wrong. Be the adult and admit it. Ignorance is not bliss, nor is it an acceptable excuse.
- *If you think your RA may have been wrong, address it with the right people.* Schedule time to talk to your hall director about it. Make sure you have a real reason to think your RA was wrong, though. Your RA went through a week's training or more on the rules and standards in a residence hall. Chances are they know the rules, and limits, better than you.
- *Schedule your appointment.* When you get that judicial letter from your HD or your dean, call for your meeting. The last thing you want is a hold on your records so you cannot register for classes. Ignoring it will *not* make it go away.
- *Be informed about the process.* Check around campus for an ombudsman program to help advocate for you and help you achieve positive solutions. These are often peers who are trained in understanding the judicial system.
- *Move on.* Once you are issued a sanction, you still need to live on your floor and interact with your RA. After all, they are supposed to be a good shoulder to cry on. Talk with them about what happened and clear the air. You'll both feel better. Learn from your experience, and don't make the same mistake twice.

—Emily Balcom, director of Residence Life at Utica College (NY)

NOW WHAT HAPPENS?

If you're documented for a policy violation, depending on the severity of the charge, you might expect the following:

- The RA or other staff member will document the incident and turn in that paperwork to his supervisor.
- A judicial meeting with your hall director may occur so you can tell your side of the story. Then, if deemed necessary, appropriate sanctions will be imposed.
- The police and/or Public Safety might be called in, depending on the violation.
- Your case may be sent to a judicial conduct board, often made up of peers, faculty, and staff, for a hearing.
- A fine may be imposed.
- You may have to perform community service hours or pay restitution for damages.
- Your parents may be notified.
- You may have to attend a class or counseling sessions.
- You could be moved to another dorm or removed from student housing.
- You could be expelled from school.

The specific judicial process is different at every school, so find out *now* how it works. And then, if at all possible, steer clear of getting involved in any policy violations. It just makes life easier.

You will have the ability to make more choices than ever in your life, but remember you will not be able to choose the consequences. Be prepared.

   —Christine Hollow Schramm, director of the First-Year
      Experience at University of Dayton (OH)

KEEP IT DOWN!

One of the biggest policy violations in residence halls is noise. Help yourself stick to quiet hours by

- *not* investing in stereo speakers the size of refrigerators
- keeping your speakers away from the door to your room
- investing in headphones for those times you want to crank it up after quiet hours have begun
- closing the door to your room if you and your friends are laughing loudly during *Saturday Night Live*
- not bouncing a basketball in your room—it can typically be heard two floors down
- walking down the hall to see how far you can hear your music
- steering clear of those late-night yell fests in the bathroom—serious echo issues!

When it comes to downloading music and videos on campus, just know the university is watching . . .

—Diane Russell, associate director of Student Housing at UC Davis

8

CAMPUS CUISINE

Have you heard the one about the student who ate cereal every night because he couldn't find anything else? I've heard about it, too, but not from anyone who's really seen it. Today's dining halls are all about choices, from the Tuesday Burrito Bar to Stir-Fry on Command. You *will* have an alternative to Cap'n Crunch 24/7!

THE DINING HALL

Some dining halls are, well, not so great. You'll be supplementing with takeout. But other dining halls? Think sushi stations, panini grills, make-your-own salad bowls, and smoothie bars.

Some dining halls win awards for their cuisine, and their chefs compete in competitions such as the Central Michigan University chef's challenge cook-off where different chefs from local colleges compare recipes. Or how about the winner of the National Association of College & University Food Services, another annual culinary challenge? One recent winner was a chef from Stanford University (CA) who won with his sesame-crusted salmon stuffed with dark sweet soy shiitake mushrooms and served with Asian salad and black forbidden rice in a flaming smoked cedar wooden bowl. Mmmmm.

In an effort to keep up with nutritional guidelines and trends to appeal to more students, dining halls are offering:

- vegetarian and vegan options
- organic foods
- low-carb menus
- low-fat menus
- comfort foods
- grab and go
- kosher and halal options
- hot restaurant trends, such as Far East fusion

YOUR MEAL PLAN

You'll probably get a college ID card that also serves as your meal card. Learn the "food rules" now so you can use this card to your advantage. Some questions to ask or to find the answers to in your residence hall guide include:

- Which dining halls can I use this in?
- Can I buy things at the campus convenience store with this?
- If I have a visitor from out of town, can I feed him using my card?
- Can I use this card in the vending machines?
- Is the system all you can eat or à la carte (buy each piece separately)?
- When do I run out of money or meals?
- How do I know if I run out of money or meals?
- Can I take food out of the dining hall if I'm on the run?
- Is the menu offered online? If not, where can I check it out in advance?
- Are prepackaged bag lunches available for days when I have class through lunch hours?

I love the concept of the dining hall. Because you get to campus for the first time, and you're deciding which meal plan to sign up for, older kids will always say the same thing: "The food is terrible but it's more of a social thing for freshmen." So we know going in that the food sucks! It's like we're saying, "Hey, Mom, I'm going away to college, but I don't really know anyone. So could you throw me a few thousand dollars? It's for peanut butter and jelly sandwiches and some friends."

From *Ruminations on College Life* by Aaron Karo, Simon & Schuster, 2002, www.aaronkaro.com

AVOIDING THE FRESHMAN 15

According to the Tufts Longitudinal Health Study, two-thirds of college students gain weight during their first year at college because of unhealthy eating and drinking.

So. Refresher from eighth-grade health class: Good nutrition helps you maintain a healthy weight, decreases your chances for disease, decreases stress, and increases energy. Your parents aren't watching what you eat anymore. It's now up to you.

Many schools now offer menus that include items designated as healthy choices. The University of Michigan offers an Msmart program that uses an insignia to mark recipes that have been analyzed for requirements such as fat, protein, calories, vitamins, and minerals appropriate for traditional college-age students.

Dining halls offer nutritional guides, such as Texas Tech's *Dining Smart—Healthy Living Guides,* which include color coding to reflect the percentage of calories from fat.

There's plenty to eat—and healthfully at that—when you just look at different combos. Try things like:

- Asking for pasta without sauce and then adding veggies, cheese, and other healthy stuff from the salad bar to make your own pasta salad.
- Turning a bowl of good soup into a meal by adding some sprinkled cheese on the top, a side salad, and a piece of whole-grain bread.
- Toasting up an English muffin and then adding scrambled eggs and spices for a breakfast sandwich.
- Getting a sandwich from the deli and embellishing it with things from the salad bar.

Realize that the Freshman 15 is a rule that's not really true. It is the Freshmen 25–30. How you eat when you first move into school will definitely dictate how you will be looking come the following semester. You must come to terms with the fact that although you think that you are going to use that common kitchen or the vegetable section at a grocery store rather than the 5-minute meal section, you're probably fooling yourself. Chances are that you will never even go into the kitchen, nor will you see a salad or properly cooked piece of meat until the holidays when you go home and you have the luxury of eating with your family.

—Kristin L. Grimm, resident advisor with Educational Housing Services at the New Yorker Residence and a student at Baruch College (CUNY)

THAT'S SERVICE!

Dining halls want student input. Yes, that's partly because the more students who eat in their dining halls instead of heading out to McD's, the more money they make. But also, dining service professionals genuinely want their residents to enjoy their meals and food on campus. And they're open to feedback. Many colleges host sessions where students discuss their food with the dining hall staff, invite students to sit on nutritional services committees, and offer online feedback forms. Other schools take it even further:

- Villanova University (PA) hosts an "Ask the Chef" Web page where students and parents ask their executive chef for information about food in the dining halls.
- UC Davis Dining Service invites parents of students to submit their favorite "recipe from home" for use in dining hall menus. They've actually collected them in an online cookbook.

HUNGRY?

According to the *Princeton Review,* ten colleges with great food are:

1. Wheaton (IL)
2. Bowdoin (ME)—mmmm, lobster!
3. Colby (ME)
4. Cornell (NY)
5. St. Anselm (NH)
6. Dartmouth (NH)
7. Bates (ME)
8. Bryn Mawr (PA)
9. St. Olaf (MN)
10. Webb Institute (NY)

—The *Princeton Review,* 2004

- Bryn Mawr's (PA) meal plan features a six-week menu cycle that is constantly revised via student input. Student surveys are utilized to determine cereal, beverage, and salad dressing offered at each dining hall. Some dining halls use surveys to determine music selections played during meal times.

- Yale's (CT) sustainable dining program offers meals made from local, seasonal, and sustainably grown food, cooked using recipes developed under the guidance of famed California restaurateur Alice Waters.

LESSONS LEARNED

I ate . . .

". . . mint-chocolate chip ice cream at every meal . . . until I gained the Freshman 15, then realized the benefit of having a salad bar handy without having to wash and cut all the veggies myself."

". . . nothing with 'surprise' in its name. Meatloaf Surprise, Pasta Surprise . . . we even had Sausage Surprise, like sausage isn't scary enough."

". . . pizza every night, until that ran out my savings."

". . . gourmet. My school is known for its awesome food—and I confess that's one reason I applied there."

DINING HALL HANGING

Everyone knows dining halls aren't just about the food. They're a place where you can spend time, get to know people, and socialize. My roommate and I would go to

Sunday breakfast twice. Not to eat again, but because the guy I liked always went early, and the guy she liked would show up late. Fair's fair.

For some people, the dining hall is the best place on campus. Food and friends! What's better? For others, though, it can be uncomfortable. If you're shy or feeling like you don't fit in, it's like middle school all over again. All those tables and you have nobody to sit with. Where do you sit?

The first couple nights, chances are your roommate will ask to go to the dining hall with you, or your RA will come down and announce that the floor is invited to go together at a certain time. Once things start to settle in, though, you're a little more on your own. You still might go to the dining hall with your roommates or some new friends you've made. But other times, you'll be stuck by yourself. Maybe you were late from class and the whole floor already went. Or, your roommate went off with his other friends and you're not really clicking with anyone yet. Should you skip meals? Nah, just go down there by yourself.

Do you look like a loser eating by yourself in the dining hall? Actually, no. It's not high school. In college, students are often on the run between classes and grab a quick bite to eat by themselves. Nobody is looking at you like you have a big *L* on your forehead if you eat by yourself. If you're still weirded out by sitting by yourself, just bring a book or notes and get some work done; people will just assume you're doing some last-minute studying for a big test. Nobody will think twice about it. And if anyone does, well, they're still emotionally stuck in high school.

However, while it's okay to eat by yourself, if someone does invite you to sit down, don't be so shy or antisocial that you always say no. And if you notice people you've seen around who look friendly, go ask them if you can sit with them! Especially in the first months of college, everyone is used to meeting new people in dorm situations. The dining hall is a quick, easy way to get to know some of your dormmates, so take advantage.

· ·

DINING HALL:
MORE THAN JUST FOOD

- *The salad bar runway.* Sit with your friends at a table near the end of the salad bar, where you can scope out your prospects as they walk down the "runway." Don't be obvious or rude—just a little innocent checking out.
- *Make traditions.* The night when they serve peanut butter chocolate ice cream . . . oh, happy day! Or maybe you and your friends have a thing for turkey tetrazzini (who am I to judge?). Gather your buds on those special nights and make an event out of it.
- *Check out different dining halls.* Yeah, it's convenient to just go to the closest one. But if your school allows it, get a group together for a dining hall crawl week. Have dinner at different halls. Check out the different cooks and facilities. And the eye candy.
- *Stupid dining hall tricks.* Scrunch up your straw wrapper, put it on the table, and add water. Instant straw worm! Or bet your tablemates a buck to eat something disgusting. Fold up some simple Pilgrim hats for the salt and pepper shakers. This is a college education put to fine use.

· ·

You can make rice crispy treats from butter, rice crispies, and either marshmallows usually found near the hot chocolate or marshmallow fluff found near the sundae toppings.

—Christa Sandelier, area coordinator for the Jester Center at the University of Texas, Austin

TRIPE AND PIGS' FEET?

Many dining halls shake up the norm and have theme meals. They'll do traditional holiday meals, of course. But check out these offerings:

- University of Georgia has won awards for such themes as Take Me Out to the Ballgame, Tribute to Mother's Day, and Circus Night.
- Wizard of Oz, Holidays in Hooville, and '70s Retro were theme dinners at the University of Virginia, and some nights they offered live bands in the dining halls.
- Binghamton University (NY) hosts *Fear Factor* night where courses have included a tofu salad flavored with beet vinaigrette, jalapeño peppers, and Tabasco sauce; pigs' feet; and tripe, followed by the infamous "swamp shake" made of heart, boiled eggs, pickles, and buttermilk.

Okay, after that last one, suddenly the Sausage Surprise isn't looking too bad after all.

FOOD THIEVERY

Some halls let you take food with you if you're in a hurry or want a snack for later. Some schools even deliver it to your room on request! But others are far stricter—their food stays in the dining hall. At least it's supposed to. Of course, the dorm professionals I interviewed would not condone this section. I don't condone this, either. Ahem. However, since I gave a speech for a communications class called "How to Steal Food from the Dining Hall," I can't claim it doesn't exist. (Maybe the food service people who read this will take it as a compliment that we like their food? Anyway . . .) If one were to do this (and, again, I'm not saying you should), techniques could include:

- Wearing cargo pants to fill your pockets with cookies
- Placing a bagel under your baseball hat (if the bagel is wrapped in plastic)
- Sweatshirt pockets for mini cereal boxes

The key is to look innocent, don't run, and walk out as if leaving as usual. And wait till you're out of eyesight to start eating.

FOOD IN YOUR ROOM

Of course, eating isn't solely relegated to the dining hall. There's the late-night popcorn, mac and cheese, Chinese takeout, apples, and the old cheap standby ramen noodles.

If you want to go beyond the basics, you can actually even cook. If you're looking for college-friendly recipes that you can make easily, check out websites for cooking. Do a keyword search for "dorm recipes" and see what pops up. Find student sections on sites like Recipelink.com,

Yumyum.com, or search keyword "college" at websites like allrecipes.com.

Add a few of these to your bookshelf:

- *The (Reluctant, Nervous, Lazy, Broke, Busy, Confused) College Student's Cookbook* by Joshua N. Lambert
- *Cooking Outside the Pizza Box: Easy Recipes for Today's College Student* by Jean Patterson and Danae Campbell
- *The College Cookbook: An Alternative to the Meal Plan* by Geri Harrington
- *The Starving Student's Cookbook* by Dede Hall
- *Healthy College Cookbook: Quick, Cheap, Easy* by Alexandra Nimetz
- *Munchies: Cook What You Want, Eat What You Like. Finally, a Cookbook Even You Will Use* by Kevin Telles Roberts
- *College Cuisine* by Leila Peltosaari

And you gotta love the cheap, filling ramen. Check out:

- *101 Ways to Make Ramen Noodles* by Toni Patrick
- *Everybody Loves Ramen: Recipes, Stories, Games, & Fun Facts About the Noodles You Love* by Eric Hites
- *The Book of Ramen: Lowcost Gourmet Meals Using Instant Ramen Noodles* by Ron Kanzak

Got the munchies? Dormkit.com offers a care package called Snack Attack for college students. Chips, cookies, granola bars . . . pass the message on at home.

Don't eat your roommate's food without asking first. Just because you live together doesn't give you or your friends the right to devour whatever is in the dorm. Also, it is often a good idea to share spoilable items such as milk or little-used items like condiments. Take turns buying them as you

run out, and use a reasonable amount. That way there
aren't three quarts of milk taking up half the minifridge
when half of it gets thrown out anyhow.

—Katherine Woolley, University of Southern Indiana grad

BUG BITES

Not to gross you out, but food and all its trappings can
sometimes lead to bugs if you're not careful. Blagh. Here's
how to avoid them:

- Keep food in airtight containers like Ziploc bags or
  Tupperware.
- If you open a box of crackers or a box of cereal,
  don't just fold over the bag to keep it fresh—put the
  remnants in a sealed container.
- Take your garbage out and wash dishes regularly.
  Anything with food on it can attract those buggies.
- Rinse your recyclables thoroughly!
- If you see some bugs, report 'em immediately. Where
  there's one ant, there's bound to be some uncles!

FREE FOOD!

RAs think they can bribe you with food to attend programs. Take the bait and get a free meal and stay for
the program. If you ever see open meetings or discussions
with an upper-level college administrator (director, VP,
president), sign up for it. Not only might you learn something, but chances are, there will be great food there.

9

CONNECTING WITH OTHERS

LIFE IN YOUR NEIGHBORHOOD

A dorm is a lot like a neighborhood. Just ask Tony Agati, a former neighborhood specialist for Neighborhood Connections in Virginia. Tony has worked in residence halls and on college campuses, and then he worked with other types of neighborhoods and saw some similarities. "The whole idea is to get connected," Tony says. "Sharing ideas, resources, and time is key when you live in a community. It's all about neighbors helping neighbors."

RES LIFE = REAL LIFE?

Learning to live with others doesn't just help you out now. Just think, when you leave college, you'll be better prepared to live and work within other types of communities: apartment complexes, retirement villages, sports teams, military or other service units, communities of worship, artists' colonies, retreats, etc.

I didn't know it back then, but living in the residence halls was the very first time I was exposed to living with and being around people who were different from me, in all sorts of ways. Most people were quite likable, a few became friends for life, and a few were simply impossible to tolerate in most cases. Guess what the real world is like? It's the very same thing, only the stakes are higher—particularly

*in the world of work. So if you want to start building your
skills in the area of "working and playing well with
others" (as it said on our second-grade report cards),
living in the residence halls is a great way to go.*

—Peter Vogt, a Minnesota State University, Moorhead, grad

Gary Rapp, director of Adult Student Services at
Friends University (KS), was recently going through old
college boxes in preparation for his family's move to a
new home. Inside he found reminders of his undergrad
days, from campus newspapers to student association
documents to notes from friends, and realized his homeowner's association meetings were now run just like the
hall council meetings were in college. "I started thinking
about how life on campus impacted me," Gary says. He
thought about how, in his first two years in the residence
halls, he "turned a corner," realizing how little he knew
about the world. "The halls were really where I started my
own thoughts and habits."

KEY TO COMMUNICATION

Communication is the number-one key to getting along
with others. Think about the communication styles you
grew up with. When your family members were mad, did
you all yell and scream at each other but then get over it
right away? Or did you never yell but let resentment sim-
mer under the surface? Were you and your childhood
friends big gossipers? Or were sarcastic put-downs the way
you related to one another? The communication styles
you were used to at home may be very different from
other people's. And you'll see it in the way you relate to
each other. Sometimes these styles can seriously clash.

Living in a dorm can require you to relearn your communication patterns so that you get your message across and listen to what others have to say. How can you communicate in a healthy way?

- Don't assume anything.
- Use "I feel" statements and be respectful when doing so.
- Identify the emotion you felt, not the other person's action.
- Don't yell or accuse.
- Try to be open and honest.
- Express problems from the very beginning.
- Be open to suggestions.
- Don't gossip.
- Be a good listener.
- Be sure to use eye contact.
- Be confident in your thoughts and ideas, but be open to those that are different.
- Remember that everybody is very different. Although you might think they are on the same wavelength as you, they might be thinking something entirely different.
- Common sense for one person isn't necessarily common sense for another.
- Be aware that there are two sides to every story.
- Try to solve conflict after you've given yourself time to calm down; you don't want to approach delicate situations when you're still fired up.

Contributed by Kim Fabbri, Sean McLaughlin, Allison Ottino, and Sandra White from King's College (PA)

COMMUNICATION BLOCKERS

Do any of these describe your roommate? Suitemates? Dormmates? How about *you?*

- **Nonlistener:** When someone's talking to her, she's IMing or into her own thoughts.
- **Close-minded:** Shuts down other people's side of the story.
- **Gossiper:** Up on the latest and always ready to share.
- **Put-downer:** Trying to make himself feel superior by making you feel inferior.
- **Sarcastic:** Always ready with a snarky comment to make you squirm.
- **Silent type:** Pretty much doesn't respond.
- **One-upper:** Only listens so they can top whatever you're saying with their own situation.

If you don't communicate healthfully, you're going to wind up with misunderstandings and possibly fights.

You need to talk to your roommate and floor community. Nonverbal communication such as slamming a door, displaying anger, or walking away in the middle of a conversation will not help the other person to understand that there is a problem, what the problem is, or how to resolve the issue. It takes two people to fight and two people to resolve an issue.

—Stephanie Hubbard, assistant director of Student Housing at University of California, Davis

THE RUMOR MILL

When people live in such close quarters, they tend to learn more about one another than they probably should. Did you *really* want to know all the gory details of Lindsay's nose job or Jamal's blind date? That's the Residence Life Rumor Mill. You'll find that people want to bond over juicy stories. It's normal, but it doesn't have to be the norm.

Some ways to steer clear of the rumor mill include:

- Not talking about other people in your dorm as your only means of conversation.

- Discussing ideas instead of people.

- Stopping gossip when it begins by saying something gentle but firm, like, "Eh, let's just let *him* tell us what happened when he's ready."

That way, the rumor about Ashley dating Brock down the hall while also seeing Justin back home doesn't have to turn into prime-time news. Don't become the tabloid reporter of residence life—let people live their own lives without fueling the rumor mill any further. After all, you could be next to suffer the humiliation of having your private life dissected over cafeteria food.

Part of it is that some people stay stuck in the "high school" mentality. In college, make sure that you are growing in knowledge and growing out of that mentality. Don't find yourself falling into the trap. Don't allow situations to drag you down. Grow out of high school and make efforts to resolve conflict in constructive and uplifting ways. Avoid partaking in gossiping, backstabbing, spreading rumors, and insulting others. Face the high school mentality in others with a collegiate view of conflict.

—Andrea Borean, a Rowan University (NJ) grad

THE ANTIRUMOR MILL

Instead of spreading negative gossip and bringing every-one down, lift someone up!

- Compliment someone, to her face and in front of others.
- If someone is a victim of the rumor mill, help them ignore it.
- Have a pizza or flowers delivered anonymously to someone who needs a boost.
- Invite someone who seems lonely to the dining hall with your usual crew.

GETTING WHAT YOU WANT

"There's an old adage, 'You can get more flies with honey than with vinegar,' and this holds true even in college," says Kirsten Cauchy, a resident director at Loyola University Chicago (IL). "There are going to be times when you are frustrated with your living situation, with your friends, with your RA, or with any number of other situations or people. If you are looking to get any of those people to help you or any of those situations to change, approach it in a noncombative and engaging manner. Faculty and staff do not appreciate being addressed disrespectfully and are much less likely to accommodate you in your requests if you approach them aggressively. Your peers also will not respond well to an approach that makes them feel attacked."

Kirsten's suggestions:

- Set up a special time or appointment with the person you want to talk to.

- Explain your concerns and request a solution, and avoid making demands.

- Remain calm and don't raise your voice.

- Come prepared with exactly what you want and why.

- Address issues promptly and don't let them build.

PEOPLE IN A STRONG COMMUNITY . . .

- Listen to what others have to say
- Explore their values
- Care and collaborate
- Look out for one another
- Speak up when something doesn't seem right
- Accept new ideas, people, and experiences
- Are honest and respectful
- Take responsibility
- Have some common goals
- Respect one another's differences
- Take pride
- Work toward the common good

COMMUNITY LIFE

When you suddenly move into a community filled with hundreds of other students, it's inevitable that your usual way of doing things will have to change. It's just different from living at home, where you pretty much ruled.

Just remember to respect everyone around you. Don't make noise, vandalize the hall, make messes without cleaning them up, or be the constant rule-breaker. It will annoy your dormmates and make your RA's job harder or even get him in trouble (remember, he's just a student doing his job).

THIS MUST BE SAID

Puking. Everyone does it sometimes, but more so in college. If you're going to throw up, from drinking or the flu, try not to do it in a common area. Do it in the toilet, sink, somewhere you can clean it up. If you throw up in someone's room, in the middle of the party, or in the TV lounge, you're going to be getting dirty looks for a long, long time. You'll also get a reputation as a sloppy drunk.

RECOGNIZE OTHERS

One of the coolest things about living with so many other people is celebrating one another's high points.

BIRTHDAYS. Make a big deal out of fellow residents' birthdays by decorating their doors, making big cards, having cake in the lounge, and making them feel really special. It can be hard to celebrate your birthday away from home, so make it an event.

CELEBRATE ACCOMPLISHMENTS. If a floormate gets her article on the front page of the campus newspaper, celebrate! If someone else just got the internship he wanted, celebrate! If the rugby guys on the floor win the tournament, celebrate! Recognize one another's accomplishments, no matter what they might be.

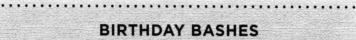

BIRTHDAY BASHES

You can make a big deal out of fellow residents' birthdays by

- making huge birthday banners
- taking out Personals in the campus newspaper
- creating a huge card out of posterboard for everyone to sign
- having a birthday cake in the dining hall
- putting a "Happy Birthday _____" sign on the bathroom mirrors
- decorating their door with balloons

Be creative, and celebrate!

CHEER FOR ONE ANOTHER. Gather a group of residents to attend a floormate's play, concert, or game. Clap wildly, ask for their autograph, or wave signs of support.

HONOR APPRECIATION DAYS. Honor the school's RA Appreciation Day or Cleaning Staff Appreciation Day. Or create one of your own.

WATCH OUT FOR ONE ANOTHER

In a true community, members watch one another's backs. Do what you can to help one another out.

DORM SUPERLATIVES

Some dorms, floors, or wings vote like the high school yearbook. Best-looking, best couple, biggest partyer. Why not vote to show your appreciation for the people who contribute to the happiness of the dorm?

Most positive attitude   _____

Most helpful to first-years   _____

Best person to study with   _____

Funniest   _____

Most likely to cheer you up   _____

Dear Abbyest   _____

Best person to watch *The O.C.* with   _____

Most likely to think of something fun to do when classes are cancelled   _____

COMMUNITY WATCH. Participate in an informal Community Watch program with fellow residents. Include being on the lookout for propped-open doors, suspicious activity, and unknown visitors.

REPORT TROUBLE. If you see broken glass in the stairwell or a burned-out light in the already-dim basement study room, let someone know right away before a resident gets hurt. Report messes, out-of-the-ordinary activity, and malfunctioning equipment.

WALK ONE ANOTHER HOME. Walk with groups of residents and double-check that no one is left behind, whether you're returning from the library, the parking lot, or an off-campus party. Be smart when it comes to personal safety and watch out for one another.

WELCOME NEW MEMBERS

Once you're feeling comfortable in your community, make every effort to welcome new members.

INCLUDE THEM. Invite new students to dinner, walk to class with them, and knock on their door before you head down to the hall council meeting and ask them to join you. Simple acts of inclusion can make a world of difference.

HELP THEM MAKE CONNECTIONS. Introduce new folks to others on the floor or in the building. Point out others who have the same major. Make connections between you and the new person.

SHARE YOUR WISDOM. You've probably learned some tricks to your community, such as where the best study room is and what vending machine to avoid. Share the wealth!

SHARE YOURSELF

"You can help build community by getting involved and taking ownership for your hall community through serving on committees, planning programs, confronting those who could harm the community, and letting others get to know you," says Waz Miller, associate director of Residence Life at East Carolina University (NC). "You are a unique individual who adds a lot of richness. Share your background and talents and experiences with everyone else, as you learn of theirs." In that pursuit, Waz suggests that you:

- Keep your door open when you are in the room.
- Reach out to others who may be shy or lonely.

- Get to know your RA and help him.
- Get to know your hall director.
- Don't be an observer, be an active participant.
- Take advantage of opportunities that you hear about.
- Make opportunities out of the ideas you have.

STAYING CONNECTED WITH FOLKS BACK HOME

Something you won't think about till it happens is how tricky it is to communicate with the folks back home. You want to share what's going on, but do you really want to share *everything?* I think not.

CONNECTING WITH PARENTS

"Your parents still see you and will forever see you as their child," says Kathi Bradford, the associate director of Residential Life at Westfield State College (MA). It's a lifelong role for them, worrying about things like whether you're eating enough, staying healthy, and studying diligently. So, Kathi says, don't be surprised if you continue getting these kinds of questions from them. You may be moving forward, but "your parents are still stuck in those basic needs," she says. "That's what they worry about."

What to do? Kathi suggests:

- Take a deep breath before calling and unloading on them.
- Let them know along the way how you're doing academically so they can help you, rather than surprising them at the end of a semester or quarter.
- Jot down things you want to tell them before calling.

- Don't feel like you have to share every detail. Think about the messages you're communicating to them.

- Don't make that phone call when you're really angry or upset about something they can't fix.

- Read all e-mails again before you hit Send.

- Share your syllabus for each class so they know when your key stress times are.

- Let them know if you'll be away for the weekend, just to set their mind at ease.

- Establish an "are we going to surprise each other or not" visitation policy.

- Call a couple of times each week instead of two to three times per day (or per year).

- If you do want to check in daily, consider doing it via e-mail or instant messenger.

- Role-play difficult conversations with campus resources (your RA, a counselor, your hall director, etc.) before actually having them with your family.

Don't make your parents worry if they can't help, but remember to let them know if anything is seriously bothering you. Your relationship with your parents will change during this period of time, but don't shut them out completely.

CONNECTING WITH SIBLINGS

Don't forget those brothers and sisters back home. Younger siblings, stepsiblings, half-siblings, etc., can really miss you—more than you realize. E-mails or notes directed at them can help ease the pain of their former role model being gone from home.

Also realize that sometimes you'll want to share more in-depth information with your siblings, but they may want to share your cool stories with their friends. Who will share with *their* friends. And if it gets too far, it could even get back to your parents.

Your siblings might come visit. If they're older and have been through the college scene, you can have fun and share stories. If it's a younger brother or sister coming to visit, plan ahead. If you invite them up for a weekend, it will be something they'll remember forever and will give them a head start for when they leave for their own dorm.

They'll be psyched, and even your small dorm room will seem cool to them. However, depending on how old they are, you may want to censor what they see and hear a little bit. You might be desensitized to everything by now. But, remember, your siblings may be witnessing all this for the first time: your floormates walking around in just a towel, the coed bathroom, the loud drunks stumbling around. If your sibling is really young, consider booking a room somewhere off campus for them. And watch your behavior, because your siblings definitely are! If you've always been their role model, don't show them behaviors you wouldn't want them to imitate.

CONNECTING WITH FRIENDS FROM HOME

Sharing the life you're creating at school with friends back home is great, and it's important to listen to their stories, too. Don't think you're too good or too busy to hear about what's happening back at high school or in your town. This may be their reality, which doesn't make it any less important than yours.

You'll e-mail and call, but as time goes on, you might find one or both of you communicating less. It's only natural, as your lives take separate directions. But it doesn't mean you can't stay really close and catch up when you do talk or during holiday breaks.

Thinking of inviting your high school friends up for a visit? That's a great way to share your lives with each other. Remember, though, what worked at home isn't always the same at school. Your coolest high school friend might suddenly seem out of place. Your high school boyfriend may be possessive around your new floormates. Take a minute to remember what was special to you before, and tailor their visit accordingly.

But be careful about inviting old friends up to school too soon. Wait at least a month.

> *The first couple weekends of school you should really be present on campus. The first two weeks of school are crucial. This is often where your four-year friendships start, and if you miss this time, it's hard to recoup.*
> —Kathi, Westfield State (MA)

When your friends come, it's easy to continue your usual college routine and assume they'll fit right in. But even if they're in college somewhere else, remember they might feel a little uncomfortable. Focus on them and make them feel comfortable.

> *Rather than choosing between old and new, try to realistically embrace changes in both. Keep family informed, and be patient with them as they try to forge new relationships with you. Realize that old friendships have to change, too. Work to make sense of them. At the same time, seek out new relationships that you believe have the potential to be long-lasting. It's by consciously anticipating*

and thoughtfully managing changes in your relationships that you will find your greatest satisfaction.

—Lyn Redington, associate director of Residence, and Drake Martin, assistant director of Residence, University of Northern Iowa

REAL WORLD: WHAT STUDENTS TOLD ME

"My best friend from high school came up to visit. I didn't realize how much I'd changed 'til we went out, and I saw how much she didn't fit in to my new world. I still feel really bad I ignored her at a fraternity party. Our friendship didn't really recover."

—Anna, Syracuse University (NY)

"I was so happy to see my high school boyfriend. Even though we'd agreed to see other people, I wasn't expecting him to hook up when he was visiting me. To make it even worse, he hooked up with my own roommate."

—Cassidy, North Carolina State

"My friend from home came up and hit on every girl that moved, got wasted and yakked all over the TV lounge."

—James, undisclosed college

DORM HABITS THAT FOLLOW YOU HOME

You know you've been living in a residence hall when . . .

- you try to use your dorm key to unlock your bedroom door
- you present your ID card for your mom to scan before meals
- you have one of your friends sleep over the whole time because you can't sleep in a room by yourself
- you move another bed, dresser, and desk into your room because there is too much extra space
- you take all your shower items to and from your room
- you always look for socks on the doorknob
- you start scoping the kitchen for hotties while you're eating

From a list going around the Internet

10

BEING PART OF THE LIFE OF YOUR DORM

It's one thing to just live in the dorms and quite another to get involved in the *life* of this place where you'll be living. Some people are the gung-ho superinvolvement types, as if they're going for the dorm's High School Spirit Award. Others come in and out, participating in some activities, blowing off others. Just don't be the guy who stays in his room studying all the time, completely uninvolved and virtually invisible, or the girl who thinks she's too cool for the dorm at all. Here's why: Many studies show that students who get involved do better socially and academically. They're more likely to graduate than their uninvolved peers. Plus, they're more connected and happier, too. So, whether you join hall government, participate in a group service project, or just attend an occasional floor program—with a little enthusiasm—your grades and your social life will thank you.

HALL PROGRAMS

A word you'll hear a lot in the dorms is *programming*. This has nothing to do with mind control, computers, or your DVR. Instead, it's a term for the many social, emotional, educational, vocational, cultural, and wellness-related activities that'll be held in your hall and on campus. Programming is what makes residence hall living about so much more than sleeping and studying.

RAs, hall government members, your hall director, and

other residents will all put on programs this year. Why should you attend any of them? Because, when you go to a hall program, you have the opportunity to

- learn about college resources
- discover that school is not all about studying
- get free stuff, from food to product giveaways
- learn more about yourself and others
- meet people with similar interests
- learn something new
- celebrate a tradition or holiday you may not normally recognize

Contributed by the program advocates in the Programming Resource Center at the College of William & Mary (VA)—Ginelle Neumann, Erica Hart, Erik Miller, Kiila Tollerson, and Julie Drifmeyer

Only you can prevent boring residence hall programs and activities. Tell your RA what you want to see and do. Better yet, get involved in the planning!
    —LaTonya "LT" Robinson, Kinsolving–North Hall
        coordinator and URHA advisor at the University of Texas, Austin

The kinds of programs you'll find in the dorms number in the thousands. You're in college for an education—get one outside the classroom, too. Programs can provide info from knowledgeable experts, fun happenings, trips, self-improvement topics, and wellness tips. Joanna Dickert, a coordinator of student development at Carnegie Mellon University (PA), suggests the following easy programs:

TIE-DYE PARTY. Dye is relatively inexpensive, and buckets can be borrowed from other departments on campus. Creativity is the name of the game as you tie-dye everything from shirts to boxer shorts to socks. Joanna suggests doing this type of program at the beginning of the year so everyone can tie-dye their sheets for the new semester.

HOME COOKING IN THE HALLS. If everyone whips up a recipe from home in the dorm kitchen, you can have a serious potluck dinner. Or just share favorite cookie, pancake, or chili recipes. You can also bring a favorite dish back from home after a break as a way to regroup with other students and catch up on how your breaks went.

CRAFT NIGHT. Get together with other students to make everything from picture frames to mosaics to pottery, depending on your interests. Crafting can be a great way to hang out while also creating something useful.

Or ask your RA if he (or you) can plan an activity. Try:

- Speed dating
- Community exploration trips
- Don't Be a Dork, Use the Right Fork etiquette dinner
- Willy Wonka night with candy and the video
- Make-your-own mosaic
- Poker night (check school rules and state laws so you don't have any gambling issues)
- Chinese New Year celebrations
- DJ dances
- Faculty brown-bag lunches
- Carnivals
- What Not to Eat, with a nutritionist speaker
- Fifteen Things You Need to Learn in College, by your RA
- Door-decorating contests
- Cultural fairs

- Staff appreciation days
- Football for Dummies to explain the rules to the uninitiated
- Planting indigenous plants around the building for Earth Day
- Political debates
- Service projects like volunteering at the local nursing home or animal shelter
- Personal safety
- Spa night
- Board-game night
- Relationship panel with couples in different kinds of relationships
- How to Get an A, by a faculty speaker
- Stump the spiritual leader
- Résumé writing and career exploration, with a career services speaker
- Managing credit card debt before it manages you, with a financial services speaker
- Laundry lessons, by the RA
- Stitch 'n' Bitch

You'll have the best time if you choose to have fun with the experience and get involved in your floor and building community. Staff on your floor and in your building will provide numerous opportunities for attending meetings, programs, and events. The more of these opportunities you attend, the more people you will meet and the more involved you will be on campus.

> —Kory Vitangeli, director of Residence Life at the University of Indianapolis (IN)

TRADITIONS

Dorm traditions are one aspect of the fun. It's all part of creating an identity, says Holly Alexander Agati, assistant director for Programming at the College of William & Mary (VA). At her school, all residence hall floors have names and corresponding T-shirts. She says, "It helps you leave a legacy, especially if you're part of creating that tradition."

Your hall might already have some traditions in place:

- Munger Hall at Wellesley (MA) has an afternoon tea—every Wednesday night. Why is it called an "afternoon" tea then? Tradition.

- During December's Dead Week at Stanford (CA), at midnight each night, students yell at the top of their lungs from their windows to relieve their end-of-quarter stress.

- At UCLA, English professor Frederick Burwick, a professor-in-residence, directs a play starring dorm residents each year. The students major in anything *but* theater.

What other dorm traditions are out there? Some include:

- an annual twenty-four-hour relay to raise money for a favorite organization

- leaving a legacy for future students, like a bench or sand volleyball pit

- adopting a family in town during the holidays

- winter midnight BBQs

- making up a dorm logo and cheer for Spirit Week

- safe trick-or-treat with local kids trick-or-treating door to door in your dorm

- the Super Bowl touch-football game on the quad
- holiday shopping trips to the nearest "big city"

So get in there and find out what traditions exist. You might even create some of your own. Leave your mark!

DORM COMPETITIONS

Friendly competition between dorms can help you make some easy connections while also having fun. Consider getting involved in or instigating some competition of your own, such as:

- joining an intramural team that plays against other dorms
- participating in Welcome Week activities such as pudding-eating contests or water balloon tosses
- putting together a dorm College Bowl or Mind Olympics team
- challenging another building to penny wars to see who can raise the most change for a good cause
- participating in a residence hall parade of floats
- holding an Eco-Olympics to see which hall can save the most water and energy

And check out these campus competitions:

- Battle of the Buildings at University of Alaska, Anchorage, is a unique and creative approach to building unity and spirit in the halls. It increases the participation of residents throughout the year by providing a plethora of events and competitions between the halls, with points totaled up at the end of the semester.

- Santa Clara University (CA) has a campus-wide carnival where each hall sponsors a different booth.
- Bennett College (NC) holds a Freshwomen's Stepshow in which residence halls compete against one another with all benefits going to a scholarship fund.
- First-year students at Duke University (NC) compete in the Froshlife iMovie Festival. Each dorm is given a digital video camera, access to editing equipment, and two weeks to come up with a ten-minute movie about some aspect of campus life. Then, during a gala premiere, complete with strobe lights, free T-shirts, and an actual red carpet, the movies are screened and voted on.
- The Intramural Cup Competition at Pennsylvania College of Technology involves physical and recreational activities in which all residence halls compete for a championship cup awarded at the end of each semester, with the winning hall engraved on a plate and placed on the trophy.
- Idaho State University's RHA puts on a weeklong floor competition with an event each night of the week. Floors compete to earn the most points and a chance at the cash prize, which is credited to their floor funds for end-of-the-year spending.

INDOOR SPORTS

Sure, you can play regular Frisbee, pool, or foosball with your dormmates. Or you can be creative. Try one of these dorm sport ideas:

FUN ON THE CHEAP

We know, the funds aren't usually there when you're a college student. So, here are some ways you can have some fun with your dormmates without spending very much.

- Read those flyers on the wall, and attend the events. Go to free movies, concerts, and events on campus. There's likely something free happening all the time. Try out something new—can't hurt when you're not paying for it!

- Enter stupid contests with your friends like nominating a dormmate as "The New Face of *Teen People* Magazine" or having a celebrity look-alike contest. Just flip through some magazines and you'll find a bunch of options.

- Check into free or deeply discounted tickets to amusement parks, movies, and more through your Student Activities office.

- Use your student ID card wherever you go. You can get discounts on everything from movies to music to restaurant meals. Local establishments want your business. Tap into those discounts for some great deals.

- Volunteer at campus and community events. If you usher for a concert, you'll get to see it for free. If you sell refreshments at a festival, your entry fee will be paid for. Give a bit of your time and you'll likely be rewarded with some cool opportunities.

- Get your floormates to enter David Letterman's *Late Night* Top-10 contests. Try your hand at simple comedy-writing by logging on to www.cbs.com/latenight/lateshow/top_ten/contest/

to see what the topic of the week is. Then, gather a group to brainstorm some possible entries. If yours is chosen, you'll win a *Late Night* prize, website recognition, and inclusion in that week's Top 10.

- Have a hall mascot, such as a big Yogi Bear doll or a blow-up doll, and have it show up in weird locations throughout the semester. Take pictures of its travels.
- Celebrate someone's birthday at Burger King, complete with paper crowns for everyone!

CHILDHOOD GAMES. For all of you dying to get reacquainted with your childhood, you can always start a good game of Red Rover, or you can join the National Red Light, Green Light League. Sure, they might seem silly and childish, but if you get enough people together and you're all in a silly enough mood, it'll keep you busy and amused for at least a half hour, if not more.

—Brianne Harrison, Macalester University's (MN) *Mac Weekly* ("How to Get Your Sports Fix This Winter." Available at www.macalester.edu/weekly/ 101102/sports02.html).

Want to know what's going on around the residence halls? At UCLA, you can turn on Res TV, a cable channel for students on campus. The channel includes student news programs, talk shows, faculty discussions, expo center programs, student talent shows, a student soap opera, computer-training classes, and student art festivals.

DORM YELLING. Yelling at people in De Neve Plaza at UCLA is a relatively new sport that has gained mass acceptance and mass appeal. In this sport, a player spots someone walking in the plaza, and then, from the comfort of his dorm room, shouts at that person before ducking out of sight. The person in the plaza is bewildered when she can't find the yeller. The player receives points for each walker he bewilders. "You might yell, 'Hey, you, in the red shirt,' before ducking under the window," senior Jessica Mackenzie said. "Then they look around and they think it's someone in the plaza. You get to watch their confused reaction. It's a tough and decidedly intense sport."

—"Dorm Sports Ensure a Memorable Hill Experience," by Daniel Miller,
  Daily Bruin Online, UCLA

What else can you do?
- Hacky sack (it's back!)
- Make huge bubbles
- Play all the games you can usually rent at the front desk
- Synchronized swimming without water (wear bathing caps and take pictures)
- Spin lots of tops all at the same time in the hallway
- Make a huge line of dominoes down the hall
- Play Twister using multiple game boards
- Foosball tournaments
- Penny hockey (where you have to hit one penny through two others without touching; each person makes a goal with their pinky and pointer finger against table; great to play in the dining hall)
- Ping-Pong
- Air hockey

- Marco Polo in the pool
- Have Matchbox car races down the hallway
- See if you can get in the *Guinness Book of World Records* by doing the world's largest musical chairs game
- Simon Says

WAIT! DORM SPORT SAFETY

Okay, some of those activities probably aren't going to be endorsed by the Res Life staff. So be careful when you're playing indoor sports so nobody (and nothing) gets hurt. You do NOT want these to happen to you:

- Hallway football is going great until someone throws the ball high enough to hit the sprinkler head. Yeah, those things really do have water in them.
- Practicing your golf swing in a bathroom ends in a broken sink.
- A dorm resident sticks his head out of his room door just to see what's going on and gets a quick-pitch baseball right in the eye—it can do permanent damage.
- The guys down the hall have a loft-jumping competition. First, it's just who can jump from loft to loft fastest; then they add flips in midair. One guy knocks himself out.

First three contributed by Jill Yashinsky, assistant hall director at St. Norbert College (WI); and Julie Phillips, former Residence Life professional. Last one I witnessed myself, and it was ugly.

HALL ENHANCEMENT

Many floors take the initiative to spruce up their environments, making them more colorful and more appealing. Be sure to get permission from your RA and hall director before plunging into any of these project ideas so that you're adhering to fire codes and other campus policies.

- Ask a tile shop for broken pieces of tiles and do a mosaic.
- Do a legacy painting (like a tree with everyone's names on separate leaves).
- Decorate with old CDs as wallpaper.
- Paint fake windows to the outside world.
- Put a frame around a fire alarm and call it "art."
- Decorate a piece of furniture (like a wooden bench or study carrel).
- Stripe the walls with paint.
- Feature your school mascot in unlikely settings.
- Buy big frames at a garage sale and paint something inside them.
- Draw the pages of a kid's book up and down the hallways.
- Put up a large piece of canvas (if you're not allowed to paint on the walls) and paint on it.
- Have art in the lounges to make it more like a living room setting.

Student-created murals not only decorate halls, but they can leave a permanent tribute to residents. I had two residents volunteer to manage the design and overseeing of the project. I assisted in obtaining the paint and supplies, and we spent several weekends transforming our lounge into an arresting collection of murals. Over twenty residents assisted in the painting process. The defining moment in this process came when someone suggested we get every resident on the floor to leave a handprint on a section of wall, as a way of leaving our mark on the creation. It was a testament to the community that we had on Hage 8, and it suddenly dawned on me just how proud I was of that community.

— Dale Barltrop, former RA at University of Maryland, College Park

GETTING HALL-INVOLVED

The opportunities to get involved in the life of your hall are endless. You can find your niche, whether it's hall government, a desk staff job, or volunteering to help with assorted programs and events. Just *do* something! When you dig in and give a little something back, the rewards are well worth your while.

HALL GOVERNMENT

Unlike high school student councils that can be somewhat cliquey, college is a time to be yourself. I know many students who were "leaders" in high school, but who were not "cool" or in the "in crowd," so their potential went untapped.

— Waz Miller, associate director of Residence Life at East Carolina University (NC)

Hall government gives emerging leaders like you a forum where you can get involved and make a difference. It's not a popularity contest anymore. Instead, it's about taking pride in your dorm and wanting to work toward what's best for your fellow students. But what is it that hall government or a hall council does? Typically, they:

- discuss and respond to issues of importance to students in the hall

- organize fund-raisers to purchase necessary items for the hall

- provide reports on what's happening at the all-campus level

- coordinate hall improvement initiatives (getting a pool table, having the piano tuned, organizing a mural-painting program, etc.)

- throw all-hall events like dances, olympics, siblings' weekends, etc.

- serve as a link between students and housing administrators

RUNNING FOR OFFICE

It might seem a little intimidating to run for a hall government position at first. Don't let that hold you back, though. Make it more comfortable by running for office with a friend or fellow dormmate. Two heads are often better than one. Come up with a catchy slogan, develop a genuine campaign platform that feels good to both of you, and spread the word. And if you don't win that first time around, don't get discouraged. Next time it just might be your turn.

Getting involved with hall government is the time to spread your wings and jump in. Don't worry if you are a brand-spanking-new first-year student—take the plunge. You'll get more support and encouragement and exposure to good role models. Training occurs each year . . . and topics such as time management, leadership styles, running a meeting, basic parliamentary procedures, and communication are covered.

—Waz Miller, director of Residence Life at East Carolina University (NC)

RESIDENCE HALL ASSOCIATIONS (RHAs)

Many campuses have an organization called the Residence Hall Association (RHA), which is like hall government but for all the students on campus. "The RHA is a group of students with the purpose to provide a better environment for students to live in the residence halls," explains Norbert Dunkel, director of Housing and Residence Education at the University of Florida. "There are well over four hundred RHAs across the United States. The national organization is the largest student-run organization in the United States."

Think of the power this group has. It truly represents the voices of all on-campus students. You can make recommendations to the Housing office on things ranging from putting up more bike racks to allowing storage for students to reviewing a policy that the students don't like. The RHA also has the money to do campus-wide programs for the residence hall students, like planning a bus to go to a special cultural event, or a shopping mall, or a historic site that will broaden their horizons.

—Waz Miller, director of Residence Life at East Carolina University (NC)

Once you're involved in hall government, RHA may be the next step. Positions such as president, vice president, secretary, treasurer, and sometimes more are typically available.

OTHER JOBS

There are other ways to get involved in the life of your dorm. Some help you make a difference—and some can also help you make money:

- *Becoming a desk clerk.* These folks typically staff the front desk, answering phones, renting out equipment, working with the mail, and more.
- *Joining the night security team.* Your hall might have night clerks who sign in visitors after the front desk closes and do rounds to ensure that everything is safe and secure.
- *Staffing the computer lab or ResNet crew.* If you're technologically savvy, share your skills with others by staffing the hall computer lab, a help desk, or the traveling ResNet team that makes room calls.

Other positions in and around your hall might include:
- chairing the Homecoming committee
- serving as the student/housekeeping staff liaison
- being your hall's recycling coordinator
- heading up the building's safety team that escorts residents back home after dark
- editing the hall newsletter
- coordinating hall study groups and tutoring assistance

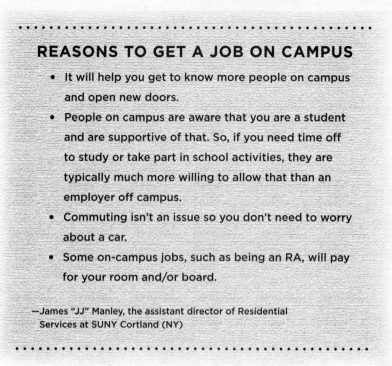

REASONS TO GET A JOB ON CAMPUS

- It will help you get to know more people on campus and open new doors.
- People on campus are aware that you are a student and are supportive of that. So, if you need time off to study or take part in school activities, they are typically much more willing to allow that than an employer off campus.
- Commuting isn't an issue so you don't need to worry about a car.
- Some on-campus jobs, such as being an RA, will pay for your room and/or board.

—James "JJ" Manley, the assistant director of Residential Services at SUNY Cortland (NY)

COMMUNITY SERVICE

Service projects in the dorms are often plentiful, especially these days as more and more students are sharing their time to benefit community causes. Do you have a passion for a particular cause? Express it and help to educate those around you. Who knows, after talking with you about puppy mills and the inordinate number of cats and dogs who are put to sleep each year, some fellow residents might be motivated to work with you as animal advocates during your local shelter's adoption days. You *can* take initiative in the dorm setting and really make a difference. Like with these activities:

- Donating hair to Locks for Love, an organization that makes wigs out of real hair for children with medical conditions.

- Organizing campus cleanups, especially during Earth Day, where students work together to beautify their surroundings.

- Adopting service projects such as reading during the local library's story hour, tutoring kids at an afterschool program, or working with Habitat for Humanity.

- Doing end-of-the-semester "stuff drives" like Bowling Green State University's (OH) "When You Move Out, Don't Throw it Out" initiative, where they collect everything from clothing to shampoo to leftover food for donation to local shelters.

- Working with dining halls on Miss-a-Meal initiatives where students skip dinner and donate meal-plan points so the proceeds can go to a hunger organization.

- Participating in all-campus community service projects, such as the Relay for Life or the Twenty-Four-Hour Dance Marathon to benefit the local homeless shelter.

LIVING IN COMMUNITY

- Lend a hand • Be inclusive • Make connections
- Take a chance on people • Have face-to-face conversations • Go beyond simply asking, "How are you?" • Support dreams • Keep the noise down
- Talk about ideas • Trust • When you're cooking, make extra and share • Carry someone's trash outside • Help people without being asked • Welcome new neighbors • Don't always keep to yourself • Invite people in • Hold community celebrations • Get to know people's names • Embrace diversity • Revel in mutual respect • Swap skills so that everyone benefits • Keep people in mind • Share kind words

and your time • Do a favor • Take walks together
• Go to the source—don't go behind someone's back
• Beautify your surroundings • Listen to what others
have to say • Celebrate people's accomplishments
• Recognize everyone's contributions • Organize to get
things done • Resolve conflicts • Speak up • Lead at
times, follow at others • Learn from exposure to new
people and new ways of thought • Share simple
moments and complex conversations • Leave your
community better than it was when you first arrived
• Support common goals • Respect differing
opinions • Confront with compassion and care • Draw
people into the fold • Be an active participant
• Become "community-minded" • Care—and let it show

—Julie Phillips; reprinted with permission from PaperClip Communications
   (www.paperclip.com)

LIVING ON YOUR OWN

LIFE AS A GROWN-UP

Survivor: Dorm Life probably won't be coming to a network near you anytime soon, but you *will* be experiencing it every day that you're on campus. Granted, there won't be any (intentional) bug-eating or hut-making; instead, the survival skills you'll develop will be real-life lessons that will last you a lifetime. You're going to deal with a lot of things on your own for the first time.

You're also going to see a lot of things. Living in the dorms might be the first time you're on your own, so it also may be the first time you're dealing with things like living near people of the opposite sex. And how if your alarm doesn't go off, your mother isn't there to make sure you get to school. And how crazy, loud, and obnoxious wasted students can get at 3:00 A.M., even on nights when you have an early exam. Hey, just because you're officially grown-ups, doesn't mean everyone is going to act like one.

Students living on campus often get a crash course in many arenas. Decision making, safety concerns, wellness issues, you name it, it's all on campus. And it all starts with developing your inner adult.

If you want to be treated like an adult while at college, then it is important that you act like one. Adults don't call their parents every time they don't get their way. Adults

*learn the correct processes and procedures for things like
room changes, resolving conflict, changing classes, etc.
Adults understand that there are situations in life when
they will not get their way.*

  —Staci J. Buchwald, the associate dean of students at Scripps
     College—the Claremont Colleges (CA)

· ·

Taking responsibility for your decisions and your actions is
a huge step in the adult-development direction. Dorm life
offers you a transition period, "from living at home to living
out in the real world," explains Rebecca Parillo, director
of Study Abroad at Ashland University (OH). "You have a
mixture of independence and structure—of security and
freedom."

During her undergrad years at St. Michael's College
(VT), she says, "I had to learn to live with a roommate and
communicate with her. I had to make my own schedule and
face up to my academic responsibilities. I wasn't alone
doing this; I had RAs, RDs, friends, and staff to ask for help,
if needed. But the decisions weren't coming from my parents. They were *my* decisions. And that was so exciting."

When it came time for Rebecca to live on her own, she
says, "I wasn't too scared. My confidence and independence had grown over those four years." Living on campus
was "so worth the expense versus living at home," Rebecca
stresses. "If I lived at home, I would have hung out with my
high school friends, been stuck in the high school mentality. I would not have gotten the full experience. And I definitely wouldn't have matured into who I am today."

· ·

This means that campus living is as much about what you *don't* get as what you *do*. For instance, you will learn a valuable lesson if

- your floor runs out of hot water because a few people took extra-long showers
- the girl down the hall turns down your offer of dinner and a movie because she "doesn't date people who she lives with" (which is actually pretty smart!)
- you can't beat the system when you're found in violation of a policy and must perform the assigned judicial sanction
- you miss a class because you hit "snooze" one too many times

ROLE MODELS

As we're in the process of maturing, it can be a lot easier if we choose positive role models to show us the way. And *positive* is the key word here. Yeah, crazy Frank is hilarious, but hanging out with him when he's trashing the place gets everyone in trouble. Daphne down the hall gets a lot of attention, but do you realllllly want to be part of the bitch high-schoolish clique? And the Party Room guys down the hall throw great parties but look how they treat girls. Search for some good examples instead—those people who are warm, inspiring, and real.

Bill and Dan had been through the difficult freshman and sophomore years already and were in the midst of "getting serious" about their studies. Watching them helped all of us "young 'uns" mature a little faster because we saw what it took to be a serious student when you had to be a serious student. We also saw what it was like to show a little leadership. Bill and Dan had the respect of most of the

people on the floor because they were "the Older Guys,"
and so when they said, "Shut the *&#* up, we're trying to
study," we shut the *&#* up and let them study. Just
being around a lot of older and wiser students who knew
how to study hard but also how to have fun, yet not at the
expense of others on the floor, was something I would never
have gotten had I lived off campus and commuted to
school.

—Peter Vogt, president of Career Planning Resources
(www.careerplanningresources.com), and alumnus of
Minnesota State University, Moorhead

So it's good to have role models, but some freshmen
latch on to someone else, almost as if they were a groupie.
You've seen the guy who has his sidekick with him; the
sidekick worships him—does his laundry, is always the
designated driver, does his dirty work for him.

When you're searching for someone to believe in, it
can be easy to put another student up on a pedestal. After
all, she seems so together, so funny, so cool, why not look
up to her? But you should never model yourself entirely
after one solitary person. Instead, adapt bits and pieces
that you admire in others into your own mode of operation. That way no one has to be heaved up on a pedestal
or risk tumbling down.

MAKING GOOD DECISIONS

Part of the dorm scene is making solid decisions, decisions that you can live with and that do no harm to you or
others. "You *know* what a good decision is," states Penny
Pasque, a research assistant at the University of Michigan's National Forum on Higher Education for the Public
Good. If people around you are making bad decisions, re-

move yourself from the situation, she suggests. The "I was in the wrong place at the wrong time" excuse won't get you very far in college!

Dorm advisors recommend you take off if people around you vandalize anything, use illegal drugs, harass people, etc.—anything against the rules. Then, decide if you're going to tell an authority figure about what's going on. Basically, if there's a chance that someone could get hurt, would you rather have *that* on your conscience or would you rather make a phone call? Even if it's an anonymous tip, you could be saving others from harm.

STUPID FRESHMAN TRICKS

Face it, in many ways freshmen are clueless. You haven't done this before, so there's going to be a learning curve. You're going to see a lot of crazy, stupid-ass things in college. You might participate in some of them. And, hey, have some fun. (I did.) But there's fun and then there's crossing the line. There are some things in the dorms that are stereotypical of freshman behavior—behavior that can be dangerous to you and to others or just plain humiliating.

Do you really want to be known as . . .

- the guy who got into a fistfight with a floormate for no reason at all?

- the girl who did a drunk stripper dance on the TV lounge table?

- the guy arrested for disorderly conduct or public intoxication?

- the girl in the hospital who took the dare to jump off the balcony?

- part of the couple whose PDA was way too P?

- the guy who tossed the chair out the high-rise window and hurt someone below?

THE NEXT TIME YOU MAKE A DECISION, ASK YOURSELF . . .

- Would I be proud if my actions were broadcast on CNN or on the cover of the *New York Times*?
- Would I want my grandparents knowing about it?
- Would I be able to defend that decision in front of a grand jury?

If any of your answers resemble these:

- Actually, I'd be more comfortable with it on the cover of the *National Enquirer* so I could dispute the facts.
- Um, my grandparents will love me, no matter what I do.
- No, I'd feel better joining the Witness Protection Program.

. . . then you know what to do.

Some people hide behind the "I was too wasted to know what I was doing" excuse. But just because someone doesn't remember doing something, doesn't mean everyone else has forgotten it. I had to hear all about what I did when I was drunk for the rest of the semester.

—Katie, University of Massachusetts at Amherst

YOU SCREWED UP

So you screwed up. You did something you wish you hadn't.
You're stuck with the consequences. But before you move
on, take a minute to figure out why it happened so you're
less likely to do it again. Ask yourself:

1. What did I do wrong? _____
2. Why did I do it? _____
3. What was the consequence? _____
4. What would I do differently next time? _____

For example:

1. What did I do wrong? <u>I slept through my psych test.</u>
2. Why did I do it? <u>I was up playing PS2 with my
   roommate.</u>
3. What was the consequence? <u>Had to go beg the prof
   to let me retake it, lower grade.</u>
4. What would I do differently? <u>Stop sabotaging my
   grades! Make a study plan.</u>

1. What did I do wrong? <u>I told everyone about my
   roommate's phone fight with her boyfriend.</u>
2. Why did I do it? <u>It was good gossip.</u>
3. What was the consequence? <u>She's not speaking to
   me. She might tell my secrets now.</u>
4. What would I do differently? <u>Respect her privacy.</u>

This may seem like you're stating the obvious, but iden-
tifying the behavior and writing it down will help you remember next time.

SOLVING PROBLEMS

Okay, you've got a problem. Maybe it's one you brought on yourself, or maybe it's just circumstances. When you're in the dorms, there's always a resource person around. Think about it. You're surrounded by people who can help if you're in need. It might be your floormates, your RA, your friends upstairs. If you break a bone, they'll sit in the emergency room with you. If you're making a special birthday dinner, they'll offer to run out and get more

WHEN YOU'VE MADE A GOOD DECISION

Here's something you probably don't do enough of: giving yourself credit for things you do *right*. With all the temptations out there, if you make a good decision, you should feel empowered and proud of yourself. For example:

- Did you study for your test even though you wanted to go out with your floormates?
- Did you say something nice about the floormate everyone else is making fun of?
- Did you help your roommate through a hard time?
- Did you clean your roommate's dishes when she had to rush out to a class?
- Did you get up for that 8:00 A.M. class or floor program instead of hitting the snooze button again?

Give yourself some credit. Do something nice for yourself, even celebrate a little when you do something right. You deserve it.

frosting at the last minute. If you need help proofing a paper, someone will pitch in. There's a give and take as you both offer your assistance and accept it, too.

But, making decisions and solving problems comes down to trusting yourself. Don't always rely on others.

> *You can and should ask for help! Are you having trouble with your roommate? Ask your RA for help! Are you having a difficult time with your paper? Ask the writing center for help! Do you have no idea what your professor was talking about in class? Go to her office hours (she'll love that!) and ask for help!*
>
> —Joanne M. Black, assistant director of Student Services at the Washington Center for Internships and Academic Seminars, Washington, D.C.

ACADEMIC SURVIVAL SKILLS

It's all well and good to focus on your spiritual, physical, cultural, vocational, and emotional wellness, but without some attention to your intellectual side, what's the use of being in school? Keep your grades up or, to put it bluntly, you're out of a job.

That's right, your "job" these days is to be a student both in and out of the classroom. Learn stuff. Soak it in. Focus on more than just grades. You have a wealth of classes and instructors and resources at your disposal! At no other time in your life will feeding your intellectual curiosity be so easy and so rewarded.

So, that brings us back to the dorms. How do you study in this space that's just teeming with life? Where can you wedge in some wisdom-seeking when others around you are hanging out, watching TV, making popcorn, comparing notes on how hot so-and-so is, and doing a hundred other things, all at the same time? You're wise to ask—see how that college education is already paying off?

But there are so many distractions in the dorm. You study in your room and someone stops by to invite you to a game of poker, your IM program lights up, and your bed is looking really comfy for a nap.

Discipline yourself when you have to so you can have fun when you want to.

—Richard Jones, residence director at University of North Carolina, Greensboro

WHERE TO STUDY

Penny Pasque is a research assistant at the University of Michigan's National Forum on Higher Education for the Public Good and coeditor of the book *Engaging the Whole of Service—Learning, Diversity and Learning Communities* (2004). She says, "There are so many nooks and crannies in residence halls that people don't know about." Find some of these out-of-the-way places to maximize your study time.

- The dining hall. Some schools open their dining centers at night so students can study (kitchen's closed, though). If yours isn't currently open, work with student or hall government to see if you can make it happen.
- The laundry room. The machines provide white noise that can help you concentrate.
- Quiet stairwells. Just be sure you're not too isolated— you need to stay safe!
- Dorm study rooms and carrels. Yes, they're there to use.
- Another floor's study room. You might not know any- one and be able to focus more.

- Out on the lawn. When the weather's nice, find a spot where there isn't a lot of foot traffic to distract you.

If you do study in your room, Penny offers these suggestions:

- Get a white-noise machine, wear earplugs, or play classical music in the background to drown out the everyday "dorm noise."
- If there's one place you always watch TV or fall asleep, move elsewhere to study.
- Do NOT study on your bed unless you want to take a nap.

HOW DORM LIFE CAN IMPROVE YOUR GRADES

You'll be living with a whole lot of smart people in the dorms! Take advantage of this brain trust to improve your own academics, too:

- Connect with students who have the same major as you do and form a study group.
- Make "library dates" with some friends down the hall on certain days to keep one another in study mode.
- Go to breakfast with other residents who have that 8:00 A.M. class—you'll keep one another from sleeping through it if you have a preestablished agreement to meet.
- Tap into the barter system—ask the good writer on your floor to proofread your papers in return for your math-tutoring skills.
- Ask your RA to invite a certain professor in for a program—it's good to get to know your instructors outside of class, too!

Students who live in the dorms perform better academically and are more likely to graduate within four years than their counterparts who have not lived on campus.

> —Dr. Alan L. Hargrave, director of Housing and Residence Life at Ball State University (IN) and president of the Association of College and University Housing Officers–International (ACUHO-I)

FACULTY CONNECTION

Don't hesitate to invite faculty into the dorms (because they may not venture inside on their own). Or go to the movies or dinner with other students and faculty. Visit during office hours, sit up front in class, ask questions, and find out more about your faculty members beyond their academic disciplines. "Get to know faculty because they are a *real* resource. Those informal connections really make the difference for students," says Penny Pasque, research assistant at the University of Michigan's National Forum on Higher Education for the Public Good.

Remember that you're in college to attend classes and get an education. Every class you miss can cost you about as much as going to a movie. Would you pay for a movie ticket and then not watch it? Think about it . . .

> —Brenda Andrews, director of Housing at Cal Poly Pomona Foundation, Inc.

FINANCIAL SURVIVAL

College adds up. You knew about tuition, and there's also meal cards, laundry, nightlife, and pizza delivery. But the biggest financial problem is credit cards.

Don't apply for credit cards to get the free T-shirts or Frisbees they hand out on campus. Each credit card you apply for (even if you don't use it or cancel it right away) affects your credit score! This can affect your ability to get auto or home loans later in life.

—Joanne M. Black, assistant director of Student Services at the Washington Center for Internships and Academic Seminars

Creditors love having college students as customers. They will often be at various campus events soliciting. They see you as bigger shoppers than older adults, with clear financial histories. By getting you as a customer early on, they hope to get and keep you as lifelong account holders. I was personally very impressed by how much they solicited me on campus, by phone, through the mail . . . I now wish I'd been more careful. I should've known some of what I was being told was too good to be true. One solicitor told me not to worry that I had no job. "Use your financial aid as income," he had said. Today, at 25, I'm still paying off balances from my first couple of years of college when I was 18 and 19.

—Anonymous, Hunter College (NY) grad

12

HEALTH ISSUES

PHYSICAL HEALTH

When a gaggle of germ-ridden students live together in close quarters, it's easy to pass around infectious diseases. Life in the halls can be one big germ fest! And chances are you already know what to do to keep germs at bay. The hard part is actually *doing* it.

- Wash your hands.
- Vacuum and dust often.
- Don't share pillows or linens, and wash them often.
- Use a mattress pad and wash it regularly.
- Clear the clutter and discard the trash.
- Keep food refrigerated and tightly sealed.
- Wear shower slippers.
- Don't share personal grooming items, eating utensils, or even clothing.
- Avoid touching people or their things when they have a cold or the flu.
- Use a disinfectant to clean your room.

—Courtney Stein, MEd, director of the Center for Health Education and Wellness (CHEW) at the University of Scranton (PA)

GETTING YOUR SLEEP

With the all-nighters before tests, the parties, the late-night bar closings, pledging, the noise in the dorms, and even just interesting conversations with your roommates, who can get any sleep? Actually, *you.*

> *Noise levels and having roommates on different schedules are the two factors that affect the sleep of college students living in dorms the most. Unless a dorm has a curfew, there are always visitors entering and leaving the building, students playing music, and people hanging out in the halls (laughing, yelling, skateboarding . . .). Basically, it's just other people around who are awake all hours of the day and night.*
>
> —Dr. Jodi A. Mindell, professor and director of the graduate program in psychology at St. Joseph's University (PA)

Have both a room meeting and a hall meeting to discuss what type of schedule works best for everyone. For example, many roommates and suitemates make a decision that there will be no loud music after 11:00 P.M. on weekdays and 1:00 A.M. on weekends. Decide on ways to handle morning alarm clocks—how many times the snooze button can reasonably go off and if it's okay to have a buzzer go off or if music is better. Also:

- Make sleep a priority and avoid falling into the trap of getting too little sleep at night and napping all afternoon. It's not good for you, and you won't get as much done.
- Try to stick with a consistent schedule—go to bed at the same time each night and get up around the same time each morning. Avoid shifting too much on weekends.
- Try getting used to sleeping with earplugs—it's a great way to dampen the noise.

- Avoid smoking, alcohol, and caffeine after 4:00 in the afternoon, as they all disrupt sleep. One of the best ways to stay awake and alert is to stay hydrated, so drink some cold water.
- Start early on long-term projects so you don't have to pull all-nighters, which mess up your schedule and can affect you for days.
- Learn your best sleep/work patterns, and schedule classes for when you are at your most productive. Try to schedule them for the same time every day so that you stay on a consistent schedule.

Information contributed by Laurel Christy, community development educator at the Department of Residential Education, NYU; and Jodi A. Mindell, PhD, professor and director of the graduate program in psychology at St. Joseph's University (PA) and author of *Sleeping Through the Night*

ALCOHOL AND OTHER DRUGS

The great campus party, that myth so big you sometimes can't see around it. Keg parties, drinking games, funnels, shots—we often expect that alcohol will play a "natural" role in our college experience because, after all, every-one's drinking like crazy, right? Actually, no. A larger per-centage of students actually *don't* abuse alcohol. It's a small percentage of students who drink irresponsibly, abusing alcohol and making a ton of noise or making a spectacle of themselves. That's why we think so many more students are drinking, because the few who do get so much attention. What about other drugs? Inhalants, marijuana, cocaine, club drugs, and speed—yes, they're on campuses, too. And here's an obvious reminder: They're illegal and their use can get you kicked out of the dorm. Or college. Or get you arrested.

Here are some stats:

- Each year, 1,400 college students between the ages of eighteen and twenty-four die from alcohol-related accidents, including motor vehicle crashes.
- Each year, 500,000 students between the ages of eighteen and twenty-four are injured while under the influence of alcohol.
- Each year, more than 600,000 students between the ages of eighteen and twenty-four are assaulted by another student who has been drinking.
- Each year, more than 70,000 students between the ages of eighteen and twenty-four are victims of alcohol-related sexual assault or date rape.
- Each year, 400,000 students between the ages of eighteen and twenty-four have unprotected sex while drinking, and more than 100,000 students report having been too intoxicated to know if they consented to having sex.
- In the past twelve months, 31 percent of college students met the criteria for a diagnosis of alcohol abuse and 6 percent for a diagnosis of alcohol dependence.

Source: www.collegedrinkingprevention.gov

Alcohol and other drug abuse on campus *is* serious. However, the norm on today's college campuses is that not everyone is drinking like a fish or taking drugs. The majority of students either drink in moderation or don't drink at all. Keep that in mind when you're making your own decisions about alcohol and other drugs. There's no need to "keep up" with anyone else. You have to make good decisions that fit *you*.

Here are some "survival tips" for people who don't want to become the victim of alcohol or other drug abuse:

- Decide before you go to college that you do not want to drink, smoke, or use any illegal drugs. If prior to college you sit on the proverbial "fence," then someone will have no problem pulling you over it. Once you have made that decision, stick with it! Hold yourself accountable. Make your friends hold you accountable, too.

- When you get to college, start meeting as many people as possible. Find out who on your floor, in your building, or in surrounding residence halls makes choices like yours. Surround yourself with those who make healthy choices.

- Don't be afraid to go out and experience life. Go out to local social events. Try and meet people from all walks of life, but do it with a friend, or two, or four, or even ten! If you're going to a club, party, or even to the movies on or near campus, take your friends with you. Friends will tell you to stop doing something because they don't want you to get arrested, be an idiot, or *die*.

- While at social events, be smart. Use your senses. If something doesn't feel right, it probably isn't. If you're uncomfortable, decide if that's because you've never been in an experience like this before or if it's because something is wrong (you may answer yes to both of these, which may mean it's really wrong!).

- If the party is getting really crazy, that usually means that (a) the cops are on the way, (b) someone is about to get hurt/lose an eye, (c) you're about to end up on the nightly news, where your parents can see how you're using their money for "educational expenses."

- If you leave early, someone will always tell you the next day what you missed. It might be a story that you wish you were there to witness firsthand, but in all reality, it was probably two intoxicated coeds (not fifty), it was a stuffed animal (not livestock), and they were yelling incoherently while playing PlayStation (not streaking across the quad).

—Matt Lambdin, coordinator of Prevention Services for a mental health and substance abuse facility in northwest Ohio

If you're ever around someone who has been drinking and has now passed out or can't stop throwing up, call 911! This is called an alcohol overdose. Unfortunately, people often blow this off. They think, "Oh, I've partied with this person a hundred times, and they've thrown up a hundred times. They've always been fine the next day." The problem with alcohol is that it affects you differently each time. You may throw up and be fine this time—but the next time you can die. If you have been drinking with someone who is throwing up or who has passed out and you don't get them medical attention because you're afraid of getting into trouble, just wait till they die. You're sure to get into more trouble because they died than you would for underage consumption or a code-of-conduct violation.

The legal drinking age does not become lower when you go to college.
    —Zachariah R. Newswanger, area coordinator of
    terraces/towers at Ithaca College (NY)

DEALING WITH SOMEONE ELSE'S DRINKING

What if it's your roommate, your suitemate, or your floormate who's having a problem with drinking? If it gets to the point where it's interfering with your life or you're really worried, follow these steps from factsontap.org:

- Ask other people on your floor if they feel the same way you do about the situation.

- Mention the problem to your housing representative or RA (they will keep it confidential).

- Visit your office of Student Life and inquire about substance-free housing.

- Get involved in groups doing prevention work on campus and get the issue noticed.

- If the problem is unbearable, report it to your campus police or other campus authority.

SMOKING IN THE DORMS

If you like to light up, chances are you can't do so in your dorm room. Many college campuses have completely nonsmoking facilities. The reasoning? So you won't inflict secondhand smoke on roommates and floormates, to prevent fire risks, to keep building facilities in good shape, and, yes, for health reasons, too.

That leaves you to smoke outside, if you choose to keep it up. Many times, groups of smokers will huddle near the main entrance to the dorm, smoking together and throwing their butts on the ground. Think about it, though: neither is a civil thing to do. Forcing people to walk through clouds of smoke just to get into the building is, well, rude—move to the side! And do you want to make the poor grounds crew pick up your mess? Throw the butts in appropriate containers. You're an adult now.

. . . .

QUIT SMOKING!
NOW'S A GOOD TIME . . .

If you're thinking about quitting, college can be a great time to wipe the slate clean. There are usually tons of resources on campus to help you out, from smoking cessation courses in the Wellness Center to individual counselors in the Counseling Center. Best thing is, these services are almost always free. There's a web of support surrounding you if you choose to make the life-changing decision to quit.

The Great American Smokeout takes place every November on campuses and in communities everywhere. This could be your opportunity to quit for good. Check out the American Cancer Society website at www.cancer.org for more info.

. . . .

DATE-RAPE DRUGS

You've probably heard about date-rape drugs, the tasteless, colorless drugs often slipped into unsuspecting victims' drinks, making them more susceptible to date rape. As Matt Lambdin warns, you can't know if your drink has been tampered with if you let it out of your sight. Plus, he says, "The number one 'date rape drug' is . . . *alcohol.* Almost 80 percent of sexual assaults and rapes nationwide involve alcohol. The first function in your brain affected by alcohol is your intellect/judgment," he explains. "So, starting with one drink, you start losing your ability to make good decisions. The more you drink, the worse decisions you make. The reason why you don't know this is true or notice it happening is because your brain is *impaired*!"

That being said, Matt stresses that "sexual assault and rape is not just a female issue." Women are more likely to be assaulted when they are impaired and unable to communicate that they're not okay or that they're unwilling to engage in a sexual encounter. But guys who think the issue doesn't apply to them are wrong—they have a mother, female friends, maybe sisters, so imagine them being assaulted. Now take that anger and enact change. Matt says: "Next, guys, think about if you or she have been drinking, something happens sexually . . . and then you're accused of sexual assault or rape. Do you remember the night perfectly clearly? Do you know exactly how many drinks you had? What about her? How clear is your future now?"

Iona College's (NY) website offers the following advice to protect yourself from date-rape drugs:

- Don't drink anything you didn't open yourself or see being opened.

- Never accept a drink from someone you don't know well.

- Always watch your drink at parties and bars. Never leave your drink unattended.

- If you set your drink down and walk away, don't drink out of it again, no matter how much it cost. Drugs like GHB can be odorless, colorless, and tasteless, so you never know if someone slipped you something.

- Have a friend drive to and from a party or bar with you, so you cannot be led away by someone.

- Don't accept a ride from or go home with someone you don't know well.

- Don't walk alone at night when you are under the influence of alcohol or drugs.

- Never get behind the wheel of a car if you are under the influence of alcohol or drugs.

- Take care of your friends. If they seem disproportionately drunk and "out of it," they may have been slipped a drug. Do not leave them alone.

What should you do if you suspect that you have been a victim of a date-rape drug? Anytime you feel strange, disoriented, or disproportionately drunk after having an alcoholic beverage, consider the possibility that a drug may have been slipped into your drink. These drugs tend to cause amnesia, but there may be evidence the next day on the victim and/or in their environment, and friends might raise concerns with the victim about what happened. If you suspect that you have been slipped a date-rape drug, you should do the following:

- Take your suspicions very seriously and act on them.

- If possible, try to keep a sample of the drink for analysis.

- Do not shower, bathe, or otherwise destroy evidence.

- Go to a hospital and have the medical collection of evidence done. This does not mean that you will necessarily press charges against your assailant, but if you do decide to press charges, the evidence will have been preserved.

- Get support to help you through this traumatic event. Certainly you should inform friends you trust, and you should consider getting professional assistance from other resources.

From Iona College Student Safety Alert online

HOW TO SAY NO

The easiest thing to know about saying no is to know that you're not the only one saying it. Most college students don't drink, use drugs, or have sex! The biggest group on any college campus making unhealthy decisions is college freshmen. Why is that? They think that is what you are supposed to do to fit in. Once you start getting older you'll realize you can fit in without being stupid, and you'll calm down.

And just know that most of the time you only have to have enough strength to say no once or twice a night. Most people at college don't care if you drink or not. If they ask you if you want a beer . . . and you say no, most don't care why, it just means more alcohol for them. If they do ask, why not? you CAN lie, saying you're the DD (designated driver), you're in rehab, you're on medication and can't drink alcohol, etc. But most people don't care. In fact, if you tell someone you just don't drink, some will say, "Man, that's cool . . . I wish I could do that." Some will start giving you their life story, like you're their substance abuse counselor . . . and the stories will go on. Don't worry, people don't choose their friends in college like high school. If you don't drink, you can still be friends with someone who does . . . and vice versa.

—Matt Lambdin, coordinator of Prevention Services for
a mental health and substance abuse facility in
northwest Ohio

EMOTIONAL HEALTH

Issues are flying around, fast and furious, within the walls of your dorm. That person over there? He's homesick and missing his girlfriend. That one? She's stressed out and not getting much sleep to boot. And him? One of his relatives recently died.

Everyone knows that college can be fun and exciting but also stressful. The academic and life responsibilities can at times seem overwhelming. And the problem is serious. In an American College Health Association survey, college students reported these impediments to academic learning:

Stress	29.3 percent
Sleep difficulties	21.3 percent
Concern for a troubled friend or family member	16.6 percent
Depression, anxiety disorder, seasonal affective disorder	11.6 percent
Death of a friend or family member	8.8 percent

American College Health Association, National College Health Assessment: Reference Group Report (ACHA, Baltimore, MD, 2002)

According to *College of the Overwhelmed: The Campus Mental Health Crisis and What to Do About It* by Richard Kadison, MD, and Theresa Foy DiGeronimo, today's college student faces increased pressures and expectations, and there are more and more students struggling with severe mental health issues. How serious is serious? Consider this: Today's college student has a one in two chance of becoming depressed to the point of being unable to function, and they have a one in ten chance of seriously considering suicide. If it's not you, it could be your roommate or your floormate in the dorm.

CHOOSE A REPUTATION

Do you really want to be known as

- the guy who peed in his neighbor's room because he was too drunk to tell the difference?
- the girl who said really offensive stuff when she was high?
- the guy being charged with date rape?
- the girl who blacked out and now can't remember why she woke up in that guy's bed?

When you get out of control, you're still making the choices, but your reputation sometimes chooses *you*.

STAYING IN BALANCE

So it's important to not only take care of your grades, but to take care of yourself: body, mind, and soul. As Ernest Boyer states in his book *Campus Life: In Search of Community,* "Wellness must be a prerequisite to all else. Students cannot be intellectually proficient if they are physically and psychologically unwell."

Any student can choose to be more conscious about their choices. Whether it be about what you're eating, your sleep patterns, how you manage stress and other mental health concerns, how much alcohol you drink, how you approach your study habits or what role spirituality will play in your life, being mindful of your choices is half the battle—it's going through life without being mindful that will put you in an unhealthy place more quickly.

> —Lisa Currie, director of health education at Wesleyan
> University (CT)

The Association for University and College Counseling Center Directors provides a listserv to which more than two hundred institutions subscribe. Richard D. Kadison, coauthor of *College of the Overwhelmed: The Campus Mental Health Crisis and What to Do About It,* queried the center directors last fall about the issues they face:

Q: What are the biggest challenges facing students today?

A: More students are facing more environmental stresses and have more pressing psychological problems. Students arrive at college feeling more pressure than they once did. They increasingly come from broken families, or extracurricular activities have not allowed them the time to build secure family ties. They worry about rising college costs. The ever-more-competitive admissions process has made them focus too much on grades. Changing social norms have led them to become intimate before they are ready or to question their sexual identity. The war in Iraq and terrorism are factors. So is increased cultural diversity, which has created both learning experiences and emotional challenges. International students have their own stresses: Asian students, in particular, feel parental pressure to succeed. Then there is the rise in alcohol abuse, which brings with it a host of mental-health problems.

Information adapted from "The Mental-Health Crisis: What Colleges Must Do" by Richard D. Kadison, in the *Chronicle Review*, volume 51, issue 16, page B20

STRESS

Stress is your reaction to a change that requires you to adjust or respond. You can learn to control stress, which comes from how you respond to stressful events. Signs and symptoms of stress include:

FEELINGS   Anxiety, irritability, fear, moodiness, embarrassment

THOUGHTS   Self-criticism, difficulty concentrating or making decisions, forgetfulness or mental disorganization, preoccupation with the future, repetitive thoughts, fear of failure

BEHAVIORAL   Stuttering or other speech difficulties; crying; acting impulsively; nervous laughter; "snapping" at friends; teeth grinding or jaw clenching; increased smoking, alcohol, or other drug use; being prone to more accidents; increased or decreased appetite

PHYSICAL   Tight muscles, cold or sweaty hands, headaches, back or neck problems, sleep disturbances, stomach distress, more colds and infections, fatigue, rapid breathing or pounding heart, trembling, dry mouth

—"Managing Stress," Counseling & Mental Health Center at the University of Texas at Austin. Available at www.utexas.edu/student/cmhc/booklets/stress/stress.html

If you are feeling any of these symptoms or see them in a friend, here are some things you can do or recommend to de-stress.

- Work out
- Laugh
- Eat balanced meals
- Make a schedule to organize your time
- Breathe slowly or meditate
- Get enough sleep
- Take up a hobby
- Do yoga
- Hug
- Have a support system
- Snuggle with an animal (even a stuffed animal)
- Take a day off
- Avoid being a perfectionist
- Road-trip
- Watch a comedy or an uplifting TV show or movie
- Call home
- Be silly
- Just let things go

I got a work-study job helping match students with volunteer work, like at homeless shelters and the Humane Society. When I saw one helping at a children's hospital, I tried it myself. It felt really good to be helping others, and I learned I was really good with kids. And it made me realize that some of the things I got into fights with my suitemates over just weren't as important.

—Katie, SUNY Albany (NY)

GO AWAY

No matter how much you like or don't like dorm life, one of the best things to do is sometimes *get away*. Living in a dorm can be like living in a bubble. Petty dorm things might seem less important once you remember there's a world away from your dorm. It also gives you a chance to interact with people who aren't your age and dealing with college stress themselves. Make sure you get off campus once in a while. Get a job or volunteer off campus, or take an occasional road trip with friends or by yourself.

DEPRESSION

Depression is a mental state characterized by a pessimistic sense of inadequacy and a despondent lack of activity. It can be caused by chemical imbalances or outside factors. It's normal to sometimes have signs of depression. But five or more symptoms for two weeks or longer, or noticeable changes in usual functioning, are factors that should be evaluated by a health or mental health professional.

Symptoms of Major Depression

- Sadness, anxiety, or "empty" feelings
- Decreased energy, fatigue, feeling "slowed down"
- Loss of interest or pleasure in usual activities
- Sleep disturbances (insomnia or oversleeping)
- Appetite and weight changes (loss or gain)
- Feelings of hopelessness and worthlessness

- Thoughts of death or suicide, or suicide attempts
- Difficulty concentrating, making decisions, or remembering
- Irritability or excessive crying
- Chronic aches and pains not explained by another physical condition

From National Institute of Mental Health, "What Do These Students Have in Common?" fact sheet on depression

THE STRAIGHT As MYTH

It's usually tossed around as a joke: If your roommate dies, you get automatic straight As for the semester. Sometimes this tragedy actually does happen. Different colleges handle the situation differently. No, you don't automatically get straight As, but colleges do realize it's a traumatic experience. The college will likely offer academic and emotional support, such as extensions, makeup tests, or time off from classes. If such a tragedy occurs, be sure to seek help from your residence hall staff and/or counseling services, as it *will* affect more than your grades.

GETTING HELP

Seeking out help is what Katie Boone, the director of Housing and Residential Services at the Catholic University of America (Washington, D.C.), calls "a sign of mental healthiness." Go to a trusted resource, whether it's a counselor, someone from Campus Ministry, your RA, your hall director . . . just go! And, Katie suggests, go before the big stress periods hit. Be proactive with your mental and emotional well-being.

"Everybody's going to be lonely, scared, and starting from scratch," Katie says. "You're all in the same boat." She recounts a story of the woman who arrived on move-in day, looking extremely polished, well-dressed, and put together. "She was intimidating," Katie remembers, "even to me. Most students thought she was really, really together." And then, a few days later, this seemingly "together" student had a total meltdown. Remember, everyone has stuff going on—it's just not always apparent on the outside.

Who can you go to for a talk, a listening ear, some perspective, or a referral? Your campus is full of people who are willing and eager to help:

- Coaches
- Advisors and counselors
- Work-study supervisors
- Residence Life staff
- Campus ministry
- Health Center staff
- Wellness peer educators

Find a mentor on campus, suggests Kathi Bradford, the associate director of Residential Life at Westfield State College (MA). "We know that students who develop a relationship with a nonpeer in the first two weeks of school tend to stay in school," she stresses. So, talk with maintenance staff, Public Safety officers, office assistants, coaches, professors, and administrators. "They're people, too, and looking for connections with students as well."

Realize that your campus is full of various resources and that it's okay to reach out for help. When I served as a resident assistant, a resident of mine was contemplating suicide over a breakup with a long-term boyfriend. She typically had been quiet and kept to herself but, fortunately, she did reach out to another RA in my building. We were then able to discuss with her the options she had while referring her to the Counseling Center, which was on campus and could help her in her time of need.

—Sandra White, former community assistant at King's College (PA)

If you're unsure of where to go or whom to talk to in *your* time of need, begin by approaching your RA. They receive training and have support from their supervisors, typically hall directors, on how to handle various situations that come up in the lives of residents.

Virtually every campus has a counseling center which offers great support for students who are struggling with these kinds of mental health concerns, with individual appointments and sometimes with group sessions as well. There is no shame in seeking out help; most students seek out assistance at some point in their college career. Counseling is all about helping you develop new, more effective ways to deal with the stressors in your life. And it's probably free—guaranteed this is the last time in your life that counseling will be free, so take advantage of it!

—Lisa Currie, director of health education at Wesleyan University (CT)

WHEN YOU SEE SOMEONE STRUGGLING

It's tough seeing someone you care about struggle with a serious issue. Maybe it's a roommate or a floormate you know well, or maybe it's just someone in the dorm you've noticed having a hard time. Rather than feeling helpless, though, realize that you CAN do something to help. Talk to them about getting help. Role-play the conversation beforehand if you're nervous. "Friends take care of one another," says Sandi Scott Duex, the assistant director of Residence Life–Residence Education at the University of Wisconsin, Whitewater. "That includes being willing to do the hard stuff, to have the hard conversations."

I remember when I was in college, someone on our floor was having some problems with depression. That person disappeared one night and both floors of our hall split up into groups. We went all over campus looking for that member of "the family." We were truly a family, both floors of our hall (first floor was men and second floor was women). We ended up finding this student and were able to get that student the help they needed to succeed. It was something I'll never forget. We all came together to help one person, when usually we just came together to socialize.

—Christa Sandelier, area coordinator for the Jester Center at the University of Texas, Austin

When I was a freshman, I was fiercely independent and had decided that I wasn't going home for a visit until Thanksgiving. After about six weeks, I fell apart crying one Wednesday afternoon, but couldn't figure out why. My roommate was so freaked out when she walked in from class to find me rolled up in a ball on my bed! I called my mom, who quickly figured out I was homesick and said,

"Why don't you come home this weekend?" After a couple days at home, where everything was familiar, I was able to go back to campus refreshed. I realize now that it was my own stubbornness that did me in, but I also never said to anyone, "Are you feeling this way, too?" Nor did anyone ask me if I was okay. It's not guaranteed that anyone else is going to reach out to you, even though staff and faculty will do what they can. But the supports are there if you need them—it's just a matter of taking advantage of them.

—Anonymous, University of Wisconsin–Eau Claire grad

BE RESILIENT

What can you do to lift yourself up during hard times?

- Don't lose perspective. It won't feel like this forever.
- Imagine a better future.
- Change your environment. Go away for a night. Road-trip. Go abroad.
- Join a group.
- Stay active—don't hide out in your room.

13

CAMPUS SAFETY

DORM SAFETY

Staying safe in the place where you live is vital to your sense of well-being. There are many things you can do to ensure that you and others in your community stay safe and sound.

> *Safety and security issues are much more pronounced on college campuses than they were in the past. Now students experience electronic building access systems, night security patrols, halls that are sprinkled, safety programs, and a strong emphasis upon personal wellness.*
> —Dr. Alan L. Hargrave, director of Housing and Residence Life at Ball State University (IN) and president of the Association of College and University Housing Officers–International

Here are some recommendations from Kathryn Keith Sims, the executive director of Safe Campuses Now, that you should take seriously:

- In a dorm, screaming can sound like partying. In an emergency, be specific by shouting "Help," "Police," or "Fire."
- Always lock your door, even when you are going in and out of your room or just going to the bathroom or next door. A theft takes less than a minute.

- Don't give anyone copies of your keys. Do not hide a key anywhere. If you can think of a hiding place, so can a criminal!
- Never prop doors open, especially fire doors, even for a short time. Anyone could slip in.
- Don't let anyone in your dorm who you are not certain lives there. If they are visiting someone, have them go through the proper procedures. You might unknowingly let in a criminal.
- Keep cash and jewelry in a locked drawer, cabinet, or closet. Keep the number of valuables you take to school to a minimum.
- Going home for the weekend or the holidays? Take all cash, jewelry, etc., with you.

· ·

Think again before you leave notes or signs on your door letting people know you are out of your room for extended periods of time. This can alert potential thieves to your absence. Unfortunately, most thefts are perpetrated by fellow students.

From the UCLA Student Handbook. Available at www.orl.ucla.edu/

· ·

- When in an elevator, stand next to the controls. Having a stranger in charge of the emergency stop switch could be dangerous.
- Some insurance companies will protect your valuables (under your parents' homeowner's policy) while you

are living in campus housing. Also, check with your school's insurance manager to find out if property protection policies are available through the school. If none are offered, most insurance companies have extremely affordable renter's insurance that can replace your belongings in case of theft or fire.

- Consider taking a personal safety or self-defense class. Check with the campus or community police to see if a free class is offered.

THINK TWICE ABOUT KEEPING YOUR ID AND KEY TOGETHER

Katie Boone, the director of Housing and Residential Services at the Catholic University of America (DC), feels very strongly that those ID/key holder lanyard all-in-ones are unsafe. If someone steals yours or you lose it, "they know who you are *and* know where you live," Katie stresses. "It's not a good thing for someone to have all that information about you and access to you."

SAFETY CHECK

Your student housing should be as safe as a hotel or an apartment. A dorm room is not like your room at home. It's important to understand all the following information so you know exactly what kind of dorm, and campus, yours is and how safe it is. If you don't like the answers to these questions, change dorms or try to change things.

. . . .

CAMPUS SAFETY AUDIT

DORMITORY SECURITY

Yes	No	Students
❑	❑	Card Swipe (like hotels)
❑	❑	Patented Keys
❑	❑	Standard Keys
❑	❑	Propped Doors
❑	❑	Doors Locked at Night
❑	❑	Doors Never Locked
❑	❑	Doors Always Locked
❑	❑	Guards On Duty (24 hrs.)

Yes	No	Visitors
❑	❑	Intercom at Entrance
❑	❑	Show ID
❑	❑	Sign-In Guests

Yes	No	Dorm Features
❑	❑	Single-Sex Dorms
❑	❑	Freshman Dorms
❑	❑	Coed Dorms
❑	❑	Senior Dorms
❑	❑	Alcohol Prohibited
❑	❑	Drugs Prohibited
❑	❑	Substance-Free
❑	❑	Propped Door Alarms
❑	❑	Fire Sprinklers
❑	❑	Peephole in Room Door
❑	❑	Dead Bolt in Room Door

Yes	No	**Dorm Features**
☐	☐	Safety Chain on Room Door
☐	☐	Toilet in Room
☐	☐	Shower in Room
☐	☐	Bathrooms Down Hallway
☐	☐	Single-Sex Bathrooms
☐	☐	Female Hall Bathrooms Locked
☐	☐	Single-Sex Floors Locked
☐	☐	Secure Windows (1st & 2nd Floors)
☐	☐	Panic Alarms in Rooms

Yes	No	**Security Patrol in Dorms**
☐	☐	By Police Nightly
☐	☐	By Security Nightly
☐	☐	By Students (Unreliable)
☐	☐	By No One

Yes	No	**Roommates Quickly Transferred by Dean for**
☐	☐	Using Illegal Drugs
☐	☐	Having Sex
☐	☐	Underage Drinking
☐	☐	Throwing Up After Drinking
☐	☐	Noisy Parties
☐	☐	Hate Speech
☐	☐	Physical Abuse
☐	☐	You Have to Move Out Instead!!

CAMPUS SECURITY

Yes	No	Campus Security Force
☐	☐	Sworn Police
☐	☐	Arrest Power
☐	☐	Patrolling Day
☐	☐	Patrolling Night
☐	☐	Carry Firearms
☐	☐	Security Guards
☐	☐	Bicycle Patrols
☐	☐	Surveillance Cameras
☐	☐	Emergency Phones
☐	☐	Student Amateurs
☐	☐	Escort Services
☐	☐	Shuttle Services

Yes	No	Health Services
☐	☐	Rape Crisis Center
☐	☐	Alcohol and Drug Counselors
☐	☐	AA Meetings On Campus

PARENTAL INVOLVEMENT

Yes	No	Parental Notification
☐	☐	For Underage Drinkers
☐	☐	For Alcohol Poisoning
☐	☐	For Illegal Drug Use
☐	☐	For Acts of Violence
☐	☐	For Public Drunkenness
☐	☐	For Housing Firearms
☐	☐	For Sexual Assault
☐	☐	For Hate Crimes or Speech

Yes	No	**Parental Notification**
☐	☐	For Academic Probation
☐	☐	For Disciplinary Probation
☐	☐	For Residence Hall Violations
☐	☐	For DUI Convictions

Yes	No	**Campus Judicial System**
☐	☐	Open Campus Judicial Hearings
☐	☐	Reveal Names of Campus

"Campus Safety Audit" contributed by Security on Campus, Inc. Available at www.securityoncampus.org/students/audit.pdf. Campus crime statistics are also available through this website or call toll-free at 1-888-251-7959

Don't drink too much, don't walk alone at night, and lock your residence hall doors. These three simple, common-sense precautions could help avoid a very large amount of campus crimes, from burglary to rape to murder.

—S. Daniel Carter, senior vice president of Security on Campus

FIRE SAFETY

Certain items aren't allowed in your room simply because they can catch things on fire. These rules are for your own protection, so sneaking past them could mean serious— even fatal—consequences. It's not just a scare tactic. After all, a residence hall fire can be beyond horrific. According to Ed Comeau of the Center for Campus Fire Safety, "since 2000, over 50 college and university students have

died in fires across the country, and countless others have been injured, lost their housing, personal belongings, and schoolwork in fires." Ed says there are over two thousand fires each year in residence halls, resulting in approximately $13 million in damage.

ASK FIRST ABOUT FIRE SAFETY

The Center for Campus Fire Safety in Amherst, Massachusetts, encourages students to ask the following questions of the Housing office when deciding where to live:

- How many fires have occurred on campus in the past year, two years, five years? How many students have been injured or killed? How much dollar loss have these fires caused? This should be ALL fires, not just those reported as arson.
- Are the residence halls equipped with an automatic fire sprinkler system? If not, why not? Sprinklers provide that vital first line of defense when it comes to controlling a fire.
- Does every student's room have a smoke alarm? Does it send a signal to campus security or the fire department? Fire alarm systems will give everyone the warning that there is a fire and it is time to get out.
- Does the school investigate the alarms before notifying the fire department? This will delay the arrival of the fire department when there is a fire, putting more people at risk.
- Is smoking banned in the building? Smoking is one of the three leading causes of fires in residence halls.
- Are candles and halogen lamps prohibited?

- Does the school have policies requiring that electrical appliances and power strips be certified as safe and reliable?
- How much fire prevention training does the residence hall staff receive? Who provides it?
- How often are fire drills conducted?
- What is the school's disciplinary policy toward students who cause false alarms or fail to evacuate?
- How many false alarms have occurred in the residence halls? False alarms cause students to stop paying attention to the alarms, which can be fatal. False alarms ARE avoidable.
- Does the school provide fire extinguisher training for students?

Source: www.campusfire.org

To prevent fires, many schools have the following edicts; consider following them even if your school doesn't require you to obey all of them. You do *not* want to be the person who started the horrific fire.

- Don't use halogen lamps.
- Don't burn candles or incense.
- Don't use octopus plugs (multiplug contraptions that allow you to plug *too* many things into one outlet).
- Don't hang hats or anything else from your smoke detector—it won't be as effective.
- Be careful with the sprinkler nozzle—hit it with a football and you'll cause a flood.
- Open-coil cooking implements are not allowed.

- Don't drape material over your lamp—that's a fire just waiting to happen.

- Don't smoke inside.

- Don't shoot off fire extinguishers or vandalize fire hoses—you need those working at all times.

- Head outside every time the fire alarm goes off— it may not be "just another drill."

- Unplug appliances during school breaks.

Some schools also prohibit extension cords and ask you to bring grounded power strips instead. Older residence halls have only so much electrical capacity, and power strips have surge protectors that will keep your electronics safe.

Gary Rapp, the director of Adult Student Services at Friends University (KS), recalls a fire during his time as a graduate assistant hall director at Western Illinois University (WIU). Gary has a few key points to emphasize based on this experience, where thankfully nobody was killed.

- Fire gets extremely hot in a short amount of time. Exit signs *melted* during the WIU fire. So, getting out quickly and safely is of utmost importance.

- People who didn't close their doors when they evacuated had soot *everywhere*. Even if they only left their door open a crack, the soot got into everything, from clothes to computers, creating a big mess.

- After the fire was put out, Gary recalls walking the hallways and seeing soot on the walls that started several feet from the ground and went all the way up to the ceiling. That's when it really struck him that "what they say is true . . . if you stay down low when you're evacuating, that's where the oxygen is."

The one residence hall fire I had to respond to as an RA was [when] someone didn't have enough money to dry their jeans, so they put them in the oven. Not a good idea!
—A former Appalachian State University (NC) RA

CRIME SAFETY

Another consideration when you're living in a community with hundreds of other people is theft. It's one thing to be trusting, but it's quite another to be naïve. Most people you meet will be honest. But not all.

THEFT-PROOF YOUR ROOM AND YOUR BELONGINGS

1. Make sure that your room door is always locked whenever you leave. In the time it takes to borrow a book from a friend down the hallway, retrieve your clothes from the laundry room, or take a shower, a thief can enter your room.

2. Don't keep money or valuables in plain view. Make sure that your valuables are kept in a secure location. Consider investing in a small lockbox. Remember, this only works if you keep the box locked and the key with you.

3. Keep a record of the serial numbers for your computer, stereo, DVD player, Game Boy, etc. In the event something is stolen, it will be extremely difficult to recover it without that information.

4. Label, label, label. If you have an engraver or if your school sponsors "Operation ID" programs where you can borrow one, place your name or initials on equipment and appliances, along with your driver's license number and state. You don't want a thief to have your social security number, but a driver's license number

can identify you to anyone who finds your stolen belongings just as well. You may also want to invest in a laundry marker to identify your clothes, sheets, towels, etc.

5. Don't leave your clothes unattended when doing laundry. It is very easy for someone to take off with items from a washer or dryer.

6. Whether you are taking an afternoon nap or sleeping for the night, lock your door. You may not hear someone enter or you may assume that the person you hear in your room is your roommate. That is not always the case.

7. Lock your windows. Emphasis is frequently placed on making sure the door is secure, and you may overlook the other primary point of entry.

—Lori Neff, former assistant dean of students at Franklin College (IN)

Okay, regarding number 5 on Lori's list? My own sorority sister went to get her laundry and it was gone. All of her clothes—just gone. The police added it to their millions of complaints about theft and told her to move on. A couple weeks later, though, we noticed this girl at the grocery store wearing a sweatshirt with our sorority letters. And she wasn't in our sorority. She was also wearing a pair of jeans similar to ones my sorority sister had owned. Hmm. We called campus security and the girl was busted. She didn't go to the college and didn't realize the letters on the shirt actually meant something.

STOP, THIEF!
Reported on-campus burglaries were a record 29,256 in 2002 (the most recent year tracked by the U.S. Department of Education). At Yale (CT), laptop theft jumped

37 percent last year versus 2002. At Texas A&M, fifteen laptops were stolen from campus buildings during the 2003 spring semester alone. Some solutions for avoiding theft:

- steel footlockers
- digital safes
- keyless door locks
- lockable furniture

From "Laptops, Tech Toys Drive Rise in Dorm Room Thievery," by Bruce Horovitz, *USA Today*, September 13, 2004

VALUABLES

Certain items have sentimental value while others have monetary value. Before you bring valuables to campus, consider whether or not you really need the following:

- that piece of jewelry from your grandmother
- a watch worth more than you can afford to replace
- original copies of your social security card, birth certificate, etc.
- your video camera
- your coin collection
- diamond earrings or necklaces
- love letters from your significant other
- important family history documents
- your autographed Derek Jeter baseball
- that portable DVD player

Some things are necessities while others are extras. Consider the possibility of theft and damage in the dorms before deciding what to bring.

LOCKED OUT

You forgot your key card and your roommate's nowhere to be found. You're locked out. What do you do? Find an RA, and they can let you back in. If you can't find one, call the front desk and they'll tell you what to do next. If you've lost your keys or card, or think they've been stolen, report it right away. Why? Someone could easily gain access to your room. This puts you *and* your roommate in harm's way. Plus, you have to turn in your keys and cards at the end of the year, anyway, so take care of it now. Prepare in advance by checking out your dorm's policy.

CAR SAFETY

If you're lucky enough to have a car on campus, consider these rules of the road:

- Park in designated campus parking lots on campus. Campus police patrol through parking lots to help deter criminals.
- Always lock your car as soon as you get in and when you get out.
- Arrive at isolated parking lots when you know other students will be there. Walk to class in a group or near other people, not alone.
- Walk at a steady pace and be alert—appear confident and purposeful. An attacker wants a passive victim, so if you walk slowly and appear to not know where you are going, you will seem like an easy target.
- Have your key ready before you reach your car. Searching for your key in your purse or book bag gives a criminal the perfect chance to take control of you.

- As you approach your car, look around and underneath it to make sure no one is hidden.
- Off campus, don't be afraid to ask store security or personnel to escort you to your car.

Source: Safe Campuses Now

STALKING

According to a National Sexual Victimization of College Women survey, more than one in eight female college students surveyed had been stalked within a six- to nine-month period. There are many aspects of campus life that increase the risk of stalking. Many students on college campuses are living—likely for the first time—without direct parental supervision. College buildings and residence halls provide relatively easy access to virtually anyone who wishes to enter the premises. Students tend to follow predictable schedules, attending classes and eating meals at the same time each day, week after week. Campus stalkers can easily familiarize themselves with a student's comings and goings, and campus buildings that don't have twenty-four-hour security provide stalkers with easy physical proximity to their victim.

If you're being stalked, let your RA or HD know immediately. You don't have to live your life in fear. More information, including a handbook for victims of stalking, is available at the website of the "Stalking Resource Center" section of www.ncvc.org.

Sources: Bonnie Fisher, Francis T. Cullen, and Michael G. Turner (2000), *Sexual Victimization of College Women,* U.S. Department of Justice, National Institute of Justice, Washington, D.C. Connie J. Kirkland (2002), *Campus Stalking,* a report published by the California Coalition Against Sexual Assault (CALCASA), Sacramento, CA.

DATING SAFETY: ONE WOMAN'S STORY

"On a cool spring evening inside an unfamiliar apartment, anxiety grew in my chest as my date insisted he would not take me home. His breath was thick and rank with alcohol. I felt tense and sick because I knew he had not drank anything while he was with me. But, his mood had suddenly changed.

"As he stalked around the room, I could tell something bad was about to happen. . . . I headed for the door. Seconds later, my feet were swept from beneath me. Time, as I knew it, came to a halt.

"My body felt as if it had been slammed with incredible force, and I could not catch my breath. Every movement seemed to be in slow motion. I felt physically exhausted. His hands stung as he began to tear at my hair and clothes. I could hear myself choking; I could feel his fingers groping at my clothes. And I could see his eyes following the work of his free hand to undo my pants. It was then that my will to live and to fight returned.

"I lay still for a moment. Then with all my might, I swung a free hand at a sensitive spot beneath his jaw. I ran from the apartment, but I had no cell phone, no idea where I was, and there was no one in sight. I slid underneath a car in the parking lot and hid.

"Within minutes he was walking through the parking lot in search of me. My thoughts were abruptly interrupted by an overpowering awareness of fear. It must have been suppressed during the incident, but fear was now shaking my body. My jaws chattered, my legs thrashed about, and my hands clenched each other.

"When he decided to go back in his apartment, I ran [for] the road. Miraculously, a police car passed.

"I cannot think of another moment so haunting as this. In the months that followed, police reports, attorney interviews, and recounts of the event to family and close friends were difficult. I cannot help but chastise myself for being so trustful, even when my gut instinct told me *I was NOT safe.*

"If I had remembered the following things, I believe I never would have been in that situation. I hope other girls can learn from my experience:

- Don't go out on a date alone with a guy you do not know well. That cute guy you pass in the halls is not someone you know extremely well!
- Never go anywhere without a cell phone. Even if it doesn't have service, it can be used to call 911 if the battery is charged.
- Always know your location and keep your parents or a friend updated where you are throughout the evening.
- Trust your instincts! If it doesn't feel right, leave immediately!

"It may have been a dreadful night for me, but I will never regret that experience. A little of that fear follows me every day, and I believe it keeps me safe.

"I will never again be so naïve as to think I am invincible. I will never again be so trusting. And hopefully, I will never again be exposed to that kind of anger and violence again."

—An anonymous student

NIGHTLIFE SAFETY

Executive Director Kathryn Keith Sims of Safe Campuses Now in Georgia offers this advice:

- *Always be aware of your surroundings!* Walk confidently and with purpose. Make eye contact with people who approach you.
- *If a situation does not feel right, trust your instincts and leave!* There is nothing wrong with making the excuse that your roommate needs you at home or that you suddenly don't feel good to get yourself out of a potentially bad situation.
- *The "buddy system" works.* Go out with a group of trusted friends. Watch out for each other throughout the night. And return home as a group. Your risk of being a victim of crime is reduced by 63 percent if you go out with one other person. Your risk drops by 90 percent if you go out in a group of three or more. It is always more fun to go out in a group, too!
- *Hold your drink with your hand over the top or with your thumb over the bottle opening to prevent someone from spiking your drink.* If you feel like it's been tampered with, call 911 and tell them you may have been drugged, so they can test you.

EXERCISE SAFETY

Safety may not be the first thing on your mind when you head out to sweat. But this story from one student may change your mind:

"It was a nice afternoon when I came home from class and decided to go for a jog. I headed toward a heavily traveled four-lane road that was on my usual route. As I approached the street, I started adjusting my CD player. When I looked up, I noticed two young men ahead at the street sign. They seemed harmless, so I turned past them and continued running. It was the middle of the day so I figured I was safe. Not a minute later, one of the men ran up beside me on the street. It startled me, and I stopped in my tracks. It was at that moment that I knew something was wrong. This guy was definitely not along for the jog.

"As I tried to run forward, he cut into the sidewalk in front of me. I attempted to run around him, but he picked me up and tackled me into the woods. I started screaming as loud as possible. I even pleaded with the man, offering him my CD player. He refused and I threw it on the ground. He continued pressing down on my shoulders as we tumbled down the steep embankment.

"When we reached the bottom, I looked up and saw another man who had apparently heard me screaming and came to investigate the situation. When my attacker noticed this man, he scrambled up the other side of the embankment.

"I quickly got up and ran to this man. He took me into his house, and we called the police. Three or four people witnessed my attack, and the community joined together to search for the suspect, who was caught about thirty minutes later. He was arrested and charged with attempted rape, robbery, and kidnapping, and he sits in jail to this day. The most important lesson I learned was to always be aware of my surroundings and to trust my instincts."

Keep yourself safe by following these tips from Safe Campuses Now:

- Plan your exercise outing. Always tell a friend or family member where you are going and when you will return.
- Avoid wearing jewelry—it could attract a potential mugger.
- Carry a driver's license or wear an identification tag. As

an alternative to carrying identification, you can also write your information inside your tennis shoe or attach it to your shoelaces with a luggage tag.

- Stay alert—with heightened awareness you are less vulnerable. Dawn and dusk offer adequate cover for muggers and other criminals.

- Try exercising with a companion or taking a dog along.

- If you must wear headphones, leave one ear exposed so that you remain aware of your surroundings.

- Steer clear of sparsely populated areas, deserted streets, and overgrown trails. Avoid being too close to bushes and parked cars where an assailant can hide.

- Ignore verbal harassment. Use discretion in acknowledging strangers. Make eye contact and be observant.

- Follow your instincts about a person or an area. React according to your intuition and stay away from areas about which you feel unsure.

- If you feel as if you are being followed, change direction and head for safe, well-lit areas.

- Have your door key in hand before you reach home.

- If anyone in a car asks you for directions, remain *at least* a full arm's length away from the vehicle.

- Locate public telephones along your exercise route or consider carrying a cell phone.

- Call the police immediately if something happens to you or someone else or if you notice any suspicious persons.

- Use a well-lit outdoor track, indoor track, or treadmill if running in the early morning or evening.

- Be sure that motorists can see you. Although most athletic shoes have reflective qualities, it is dangerous to exercise in the early morning or late evening without the benefit of reflective materials on your clothing as well.

Okay, don't let this section make you so totally paranoid that you stay indoors with the door locked for the rest of your life. Just remember to stay alert and be smart about what you're doing. Your safety is important to many people, but when it comes down to it, it's up to *you*.

BACK-POCKET SURVIVAL TOOLS

- Carry the numbers for local cab companies in your wallet, just in case.
- Memorize the number for Public Safety and your dorm's front desk, for emergencies.
- If you think a friend is too drunk, get help immediately. Don't worry about anyone "getting in trouble."
- If you smell smoke, gas, or something else out of the ordinary, report it right away. You never know.
- If you lose your keys, ID, license, or another important document, report it immediately. Don't let anyone steal your identity.
- See someone who looks suspicious? If in doubt, report it now.
- If you get obscene phone calls, write down the date and time and what was said. Then, tell your RA.

14

MOVING ON OR
MOVING OUT

Time to leave. Maybe you've had a great year in the
dorms, but summer break or a new year is approaching,
and you've decided to move on. You may be reading this
well ahead of time, but either bookmark it for later or
read now to get advance notice on what's to come. (Of
course, you can also keep this book around for reference
all year!)

PREPARING TO LEAVE

"The last thing on your mind when you're first thinking
about the residence halls may be properly checking out of
your space," says Danyale Ellis, a residence manager at Indiana University, Bloomington, "but residence hall ad-
ministrative staff must, at times, transition residence hall
spaces very quickly due to various conferences staying in
the halls during the summer." To ensure that there are no
"surprise charges" placed on your bursar bill, she suggests
you do the following:

CONTACT YOUR RA THE WEEK BEFORE FINALS. Find
out the specific guidelines for properly checking out of
your room. Some institutions go the self-check-out route
where you complete a form, leave it in your room, and return the room key to your residence hall desk. Other
places require that you set up a time with your RA so he
can check you out of your room, making sure there are

no damages and that you've left everything clean. Which leads us to . . .

CLEAN YOUR ROOM. Students are charged every year within the residence halls for hours of excessive cleaning because they don't do a few simple things. So, take the time to sweep and mop your floor, and remove all your belongings from the dresser, closet, and desk. Make sure that you check under the bed as something important may have slipped under there. And make sure that you have removed tape or any other adhesive materials from the walls. The charges for wall damages can sometimes be hundreds of dollars.

CONTRIBUTE TO FOOD AND CLOTHING DRIVES. Packing to leave while studying for finals can become overwhelming, so a large number of students just end up trashing food, clothes, and other items that they can't find room for or no longer need. Instead of trashing these valuable items, consider donating them to a worthy organization. Many dorms sponsor end-of-the-year food and clothing drives and will have drop-off locations. Talk with your RA about what's available or check your floor's bulletin board for information.

CHUCK YOUR GARBAGE. That broken drying rack or mangled hamper may not be going home with you. Take large items like these directly to the large Dumpsters outside instead of leaving them in common areas, please! Also encourage other residents to do the same so that none of you have to face common-area cleaning charges.

OFFICIALLY CHECK OUT OF YOUR SPACE. Follow the checkout guidelines outlined by your RA. Sign the room condition report that details what condition you left your room in. Make sure that areas not shared with your room-mate (if applicable) are noted as well as who checked out first (you don't want to be held responsible for a hole in the wall that happens *after* you check out!). Discuss any damages with your RA. Then, get a copy of the room condition form to take home with you. Off to summer break you go!

IF YOU'RE BREAKING YOUR HOUSING CONTRACT

At most colleges and universities, the housing agreement is a legally binding contract. It can be harder to get out of some contracts than others. Releases are sometimes granted only under extenuating circumstances, such as leaving school, marriage, studying abroad, or hospitalization.

If you really need to break your contract and Residence Life won't grant your request, try talking to a higher authority (dean of students, director of Residence Life); this also might be an appropriate time to involve your parents and have them make the contact. As a final resort, you might seek legal advice.

CHOOSING WHERE TO LIVE NEXT YEAR

When it's time to start planning for next year, you've got some options:

- staying where you are with your current roommate(s)
- staying in your dorm with a different roommate(s) of your choice
- staying in your dorm and using the roommate lottery to choose a new roommate for you
- moving to a new dorm with your roommate
- moving off campus into an apartment with whatever roommates you choose

The decision is completely up to you. Think about what worked in the past and what you'd want changed in the future. Don't assume your current roommate is staying in place. Ask what her plans are, so you're not caught off guard if she's planning to leave.

You'll likely need to go through a housing-lottery process if you plan to stay somewhere on campus next year. You can't avoid this process if your school does one—you'll be without housing if you just blow it off. So, ask questions and go to those "Lottery Info Meetings" so you can better understand terms like *squatters* (students who want to stay in their same room next year). Check out theme houses, living-learning communities, upperclass housing, and more so you can have a few options. Remember, you won't always be guaranteed your first choice, so it's smart to have a Plan B.

Most housing lotteries happen early in the spring semester. Watch for signs, go to floor meetings, and read e-mails/ flyers from the office of Residence Life. It's up to you to get informed! Don't let this process sneak up on you, which could leave you scrambling around the night before the lottery, trying to find a roommate when everyone else has already figured out what they're doing. Get the conversations rolling before winter break so you're fully prepared. And remember, your housing lottery number can be based on your class year, your academic standing, your judicial record, or a mixture of those things. Actions have consequences, even when it comes to choosing your room. Good behavior is rewarded.

CONSIDERING OFF-CAMPUS HOUSING

If you're not required to live on campus, you may be interested in exploring off-campus options. Before you do, just ask yourself a few simple questions:

- What will my transportation situation be? Can I rely on public transportation? Do I want to contend with campus parking if I have my own car?
- Am I ready to live with one or just a few roommates or do I still want to meet a bunch of new people?
- If I come to campus for class in the morning, will I be stuck on campus all day/night because my classes and involvements are so spread out?
- How will this impact me financially? Is any part of my financial aid and/or scholarship money tied in to living on campus?
- Will I really cook for myself if I move off campus? Will I be able to eat well and stay healthy?
- Can I handle paying rent and bills on time?
- Am I ready to buy furnishings?
- Will I be as involved as I want on campus if I have to leave campus to go home at night?
- What will I miss about living on campus? Are there enough trade-offs?

CHERISHING YOUR DORM MEMORIES

Whether you're leaving the dorms for good or just for summer break, take some time to reflect. When it comes time to say good-bye to your community, it can be tough after all you've shared and how you've changed. When you ask people to tell you about college, chances are they'll remember some of their dorm experiences for a long, long time.

So wrap it up right; you want to take the memories with you. Julie Phillips, a former Residence Life professional at various colleges, suggests:

TAKE A FLOOR PHOTO. Have your RA help you set this up. Ask everyone to dress alike, in flannel shirts, pajamas, or floor T-shirts. Or see if they'll wear the craziest pattern combinations possible for a very colorful picture. Then, get a group shot you're bound to treasure for many years to come.

MAKE CLIPBOARD COLLAGES. Ask everyone to save old magazines and catalogs during the last month or so. Then, on a Sunday afternoon toward the end of the year, invite folks to the lounge, asking them to bring scissors. See if your RA will help you get glue and a clipboard for each person. Hang out, playing good music and talking while you cut out stuff from the old magazines that remind you of different people on your floor. Pass these clippings to the appropriate people—it'll show them the positive things that others think about them! Then, encourage everyone to make their own collage of clippings on the back of their clipboards for a useful tool that is also full of memories.

MAKE A QUOTE BOARD. On the common bathroom or lounge door, tack up a "Quotes of the Year" board where everyone can jot the funny, meaningful, embarrassing things they've said throughout the year.

PLANT TULIPS OR A TREE. Get permission to plant tulips or a tree outside your hall, complete with a plaque saying something like "From Third-Floor Waterbury Hall."

MAKE A BIRTHDAY BOOK. See if your RA has everyone's birthdays or gather your own list. E-mail it to everyone, along with a link to a birthday reminder site like www.birthdayalarm.com. This will help you remember your floormates when you no longer see them on a day-to-day basis.

CREATE A FLOOR COLLAGE. Ask your RA if you can use a floor bulletin board or wall space. Then, encourage people to put up words, photos, anything that reminds them of the year, whether it's a ticket to the campus Green Day concert or a letter from the hall director, thanking your floor for having the least floor damage. Take a digital photo of the completed collage and e-mail it to everyone so they have their own memento of the year.

LIST THE "YEAR IN REVIEW." Make a floor list of all the funny, sad, caring, weird memories you can think of, from the late-night Shamrock Shake run to the big intradorm snowball fight. The Year in Review will help you remember it all.

TAKE A CLIPPING. At the beginning of the year, get a big spider plant or some other easy-to-care-for plant. Leave it in the lounge or the bathroom (with permission, of course), encouraging folks to take care of it together. At the end of the year, have a ceremony where everyone can take a clipping from the same plant to start their own plant. It'll symbolize how your community has "grown" over the past year and allow you all to take a piece of that with you, wherever you may go.

GET YOURSELF SOME FLOORWEAR. Everyone makes hall T-shirts, which can definitely be fun. Why not think outside of the box, though, and create some other kind of floorwear, too? Make it floor baseball caps or knit hats or flannel pants or backpacks or blankets—sky's the limit!

CREATE A FLOOR DVD. Gather digital photos, video, and more from other residents that you can turn into a slideshow of sorts. Toss in some good tunes and a fancy cover and you have the ultimate keepsake.

MAKE PICTURE FRAMES. Get a gaggle of plastic frames and paint pens and go to town, with everyone making their own picture-frame creations (or everyone making another person's) that you can use to display your floor photo.

LIST "OUR RULES OF LIFE." Ask each student to submit five to ten of their "Rules of Life," whether it's "Look both ways before crossing the street" or "Do something that scares you at least once a month." List all of these in one document and then get it blown up poster-size. Everyone will have a "Rules of Life" poster from the floor to take with them when they leave the group.

LEAVE A LEGACY. Consider leaving some sort of gift for the group of students who will live in your community next year. It can be a cool framed poster for the common lounge, a Cranium game to share, a paper-towel dispenser in the bathroom, a meaningful mural, or some other mark of distinction that will help your community spirit live on, long after you all leave. Pass the torch.

RECORD YOUR OWN PERSONAL MEMORIES IN A SCRAP-BOOK OR PHOTO ALBUM. Fill out the Dorm Memories Journal on the following pages as you go through the year, and include it in your scrapbook. It will be fun to look back on someday, when you're living in your mansion/penthouse/peace corps hut/beach house with your spouse/partner/kids/dog/same roommate you've had all along.

Dorm Memories Journal

What were your first impressions of your dorm?

What were your first impressions of your room?

What were your first impressions of your roommate?

What was the most surprising thing about your roommate?

Draw a picture of your dorm room.

What was your view out the window?

Who moved you in?

What happened the first day you were there?

What should you have left at home?

What was the most surprising thing about living in the dorm?

Who was your RA? What did you think of him or her?

Who was your best friend in the dorm?

What was the funniest thing that happened in the dorm?

What was the weirdest thing that happened in the dorm?

What was the grossest thing that happened in the dorm?

What was the best program you attended?

What will you miss most about living in the dorms?

List some of the memories you want to take with you.

Acknowledgments

I met Julie Phillips in seventh grade. We went to high school together and then to the same college where we both lived in the dorms. After that, we went our separate ways. Then I heard that Julie was in the college residence hall business, and we reconnected. She was invaluable in contacting Residence Life people for this book! So, a huge thank-you to Julie, the assistant publisher for Editorial at PaperClip Communications!

And thanks to . . .

All the dedicated residence hall professionals and students who generously gave such awesome information.

My editor at Three Rivers Press, Lindsey Moore, and the book's original editors, Orly Trieber and Denise Sternad. And everyone in editorial, promotion, sales, marketing, and production at Random House, especially Carrie Thornton, Steve Ross, Jenny Frost, Camille Smith, Elina Nudelman, Leta Evanthes, and Arin Lawrence.

My agents Sue Cohen and Rebecca Sherman at Writers House Literary Agency and Andy McNichol at William Morris Agency.

My family: my husband, David DeVillers, whom I first met in my freshman dorm. My kids, Quinn and Jack. My sisters Jennifer Roy and Amy Rozines. My mom, Robin Rozines. The DeVillers family.

Melissa Wiechmann from BYou, Johannah Haney, Meg Cabot, and Aaron Karo at Aaronkaro.com.

I had a lot of flashbacks to my own dorm days at SUNY Oswego. And I've got proof that those friendships last in my own friends Jacki, Carol, Melanie, Sue, and Christine.

INDEX

About the Author

Julia DeVillers is the author of fiction and nonfiction books, including *Girlwise: How to Be Confident, Capable, Cool, and In Control* and *How My Private, Personal Journal Became a Bestseller.* She lives in Columbus, Ohio. Her website is www.girl wise.com.